MIDLOTHIAN
PUBLIC LIBRARY

BURQAS, BASEBALL,
AND APPLE PIE

ALSO BY RANYA TABARI IDLIBY

The Faith Club: A Muslim, A Christian, A Jew—
Three Women Search for Understanding

BURQAS, BASEBALL, AND APPLE PIE

BEING MUSLIM
IN AMERICA

RANYA TABARI IDLIBY

palgrave
macmillan

First published in 2014 by PALGRAVE MACMILLAN® in the United
States—a division of St. Martin's Press LLC, 175 Fifth Avenue, New York,
NY 10010.

Where this book is distributed in the UK, Europe and the rest of the
world, this is by Palgrave Macmillan, a division of Macmillan Publishers
Limited, registered in England, company number 785998, of Houndmills,
Basingstoke, Hampshire RG21 6XS.

Palgrave Macmillan is the global academic imprint of the above companies
and has companies and representatives throughout the world.

Palgrave® and Macmillan® are registered trademarks in the United States,
the United Kingdom, Europe and other countries.

ISBN: 978-0-230-34184-5

Library of Congress Cataloging-in-Publication Data

Idliby, Ranya, 1965–
  Burqas, baseball, and apple pie : being Muslim in America / Ranya Tabari
Idliby.
  pages   cm
   ISBN 978-0-230-34184-5 (hardback : alkaline paper)
   1. Idliby, Ranya, 1965- 2. Idliby, Ranya, 1965—Family. 3. Muslim
families—United States. 4. Muslims—United States—Ethnic identity.
5. Islamophobia—United States. 6. Muslims—Cultural assimilation—
United States. 7. Muslims—United States—Social conditions. 8. United
States—Ethnic relations. 9. United States—Social conditions—1980–
10. United States—Religious life and customs. I. Title.
E184.M88I35   2014
305.6'97073—dc23
                                                          2013036413

A catalogue record of the book is available from the British Library.

Design by Letra Libre Inc.

First edition: January 2014

10 9 8 7 6 5 4 3 2 1

Printed in the United States of America.

For

my mother's faith,
my father's reason,
and
my faith and reason in life:
Leia, Taymor, and Sami

* * *

"One who lives forty days among a people becomes
one of them."

—Muslim proverb

CONTENTS

8 pages of photographs appear between pages 118 and 119.

ACKNOWLEDGMENTS

THANK YOU ELIZABETH KAPLAN FOR YOUR perseverance, patience, and critical input during the early stages of the manuscript, without you there would be no book. Thank you Karen Wolny for seeing what others did not foresee. Thank you Adrienne Hart for your help editing, but most importantly for our late-night conversations and your emotional support. Thank you to the publishing team at Palgrave Macmillan, who worked hard on producing and marketing this book. Thank you to all those who have ever believed in me and who continue to support me, you know who you are. Finally, thank you Leia and Taymor, for being my pride, my joy, and my daily inspiration.

PROLOGUE

"HOW DARE YOU SIT HERE AND NOT APOLO-
gize for 9/11?" an older, distinguished-looking gentleman demanded to know at the end of the Q&A session for a presentation
of my book *The Faith Club*. I took a deep breath, willed my beating heart to slow, and desperately held on to what I hoped was a
warm, empathetic smile as I bit down my mounting panic. I was
a seasoned public speaker by then: as the American Muslim co-
author of the *New York Times* bestseller *The Faith Club*, I had been
welcomed in scores of communities across America as part of an
extended book tour. What had started out as an intimate interfaith conversation in the privacy of our homes had been blessed
with an enduring and rewarding public voice. Over three years,
America had become one large Faith Club. My Faith Club co-
authors, Suzanne and Priscilla, and I crisscrossed the country from
the mountains of Boise, Idaho, to the shores of Jacksonville, Florida. We were embraced in dozens of churches, temples, mosques,
universities, and seminaries, and I had learned to anticipate the

most difficult of questions. As the last speaker in our three-way presentation, I always signed off with our Faith Club mantra: "We at the Faith Club are not for editing our language but for enlightening our thoughts. So please feel free to ask us any questions on your mind. Don't be shy." We were in Omaha when the question I had never been asked before, never anticipated, came my way. This man's barrage took on a personal note, and I could feel Priscilla and Suzanne lean protectively closer to me as he delivered his final verdict: "Your people are the source of violence all over the world." "My people are your people," I assured him, naively hoping that he would change his mind once I revealed our shared patriotism. "I am an American too." "Oh no you are not!" he fired back. Eventually, an event organizer caught on to the exchange and helped diplomatically usher my vocal assailant away. The following morning, en route to Boise, Idaho, I received an apologetic phone call from the event organizers, who graciously arranged for a large bouquet of birds of paradise flowers to be delivered to my hotel room. I was appreciative of the gesture even though I was more frazzled than offended.

My birds of paradise could not mask a sobering reality: the hyphenated identity of my American-Muslim family is not without its determined detractors. For many Americans, the words "American" and "Muslim" simply do not marry well; for many the combination is an anathema, a contradiction in values, loyalties, and identities. It may well take my children a lifetime to make peace with the two components of their identities. A 2006 *USA*

Today/Gallup poll found that less than half of Americans believe that American Muslims are loyal to the United States, and nearly one-quarter say they would not want a Muslim as a neighbor.[1] According to a 2010 *Time* magazine poll, 28 percent of Americans do not believe that Muslims should be eligible to sit on the United States Supreme Court, and nearly one-third think they should be banned from running for president.[2] A 2010 poll reported that 53 percent of Americans had either a "not favorable at all" or a "not too favorable opinion" of Islam.[3] According to the *New York Times,* in 2006 the Department of Homeland Security signed a $385 million contract with a subsidiary of Halliburton to build emergency detention facilities, each capable of holding five thousand people, to accommodate an emergency influx of immigrants or to support the "rapid development of new programs." When asked to elaborate on what type of new programs, officials declined to do so, leaving many speculating on the possibility that they may be used to detain American Muslim citizens in the aftermath of another 9/11-like terrorist attack.[4] Growing up in this environment is not without its challenges. Headline news, political campaigns, and events that are completely out of our control intrude, more often than we care for, on our family dinners and conversations.

This is the story of one American Muslim family. The story of how through our lives, our schools, our friends and neighbors, we end up living the challenges, myths, fears, hopes, and dreams of all Americans. We are challenged both by Muslims who speak for us and by Americans who reject us. We have far too often found ourselves at a loss for words, wrestling equally with issues from within the faith and the stereotypes that continue to flourish outside it. We have had to learn and relearn what it means to be American and Muslim today. Yet we refuse to give up on either. Through it all, we have chosen to speak up, to value and honor both. We have chosen love, patriotism, and faith over hate, alienation, and disillusionment. We are mothers, fathers, sons, and daughters. Our hopes and challenges are America's own. In spite of—and in defiance of—all the naysayers, we remain American, Muslim, and proud.

ONE

Why Would Anyone Choose to Be a Muslim?

He who chooses to enter Paradise through its best door must please
his parents.
Paradise lies at the feet of your mother.

—The Prophet Muhammad[1]

WALKING HOME FROM A FRIEND'S HOUSE ONE day, my ten-year-old son spotted a poster of the legendary boxer Muhammad Ali and told me how disappointed he was to find out that Ali was not a real Muslim, but a convert. "Don't be silly," I said, thinking I had this parenting moment completely under control. "When a person chooses to convert, it may be even more meaningful. It means they have thought about their religion and made it their personal choice, not just an accident of birth." I was not ready for his quick and shocking retort: "Why would *anyone choose* to be a Muslim?"

Being Muslim in America was not always the challenge it seems to be for my children today. At sixteen, my father, a Palestinian refugee, was given a one-way ticket to the United States by his father. His mission was to get an education. He landed in Chicago and worked his way through college. It took him ten years, but he graduated with a double major in math and engineering from the University of Illinois. He worked on the docks and held down a second job at a cafeteria where he enjoyed flirting with the sorority girls. He often faced the brutal Chicago cold without the luxury of the coat he shared with his older brother and cousin. Whoever was up first in the morning was warm for the day. Nothing in his early, pampered childhood could possibly have prepared my father for his new life. He was the privileged son of a medical doctor whose landed wealth was lost with the loss of Palestine. His father, Dr. Rashid, could not even afford to buy my father a ticket back to Jordan when my father's mother, the renowned beauty of Tiberius, died at the age of thirty-eight. Medically, she died of kidney failure, but family lore insists that she died from the heartache of loss. My father would not learn of her death until he returned home as a graduate at the age of twenty-six.

The decade in Chicago turned my father into the man he remains today. He learned the humility of hunger: when desperate for nutrition, he rummaged through the butcher's discarded scraps in search of shanks for a stew that would accompany his staple food: rice. Chicago's lessons he learned for life: hard work, discipline, self-reliance, and an aversion to waste and the mockery of overpriced luxury goods. A spendthrift he would never become, even as he single-handedly turned his fortunes around. Self-made, he demanded the same work ethic from his children, and promoted the values of discipline and hard work.

At nineteen my fair, green-eyed mother fell in love with the dashingly handsome, exotically Americanized engineer to whom she was introduced by a family friend. By twenty, she had married him, and I was well on the way. If food is love, then my mother was madly in love. As a young mother she spent hours baking and cooking, perfecting recipes from her cherished Betty Crocker cookbook. I can still see her studiously leafing through its pages. Cookbooks were like novels to her, and with their recipes she would knead narratives into her young family's life. Around the table we could travel and share and love. Before we could afford to make our first trip to the States from our then current home in Kuwait, we had already traveled there by way of my mother's prolific kitchen. Apple pies, lemon meringue pies, cheesecakes, homemade doughnuts, and banana splits were shared as a celebration of my father's past American life. For a more traditional narrative, especially on religious holidays, we enjoyed homemade pistachio-filled butter cookies, date cookies, apricot and cream custards, and honeyed-almond and hazelnut cakes.

My father, more secular than my mother, left it up to her to ground us in our faith. We were Muslims living in a Muslim country. If I felt a sense of being "other," it was about being Palestinian and living in Kuwait. Our Islam was full of joy and celebration, like the Eid Feast at the end of the Holy Month of fasting known as Ramadan. Eid was my favorite Muslim holiday. For an entire month my mother would fast from sunrise to sunset. My father did not fast but would give up alcohol in deference to the holiness of the month: a month of reflection, worship, charity, and prayer. I was not allowed to fast because my growing body needed nourishment, but I was encouraged to share in the spirit of the month by giving up an indulgence or helping out a friend. At dusk my brother and I were sent out to the garden, eager scouts listening carefully for the thunder of the canon, set off daily to signal the end of a day's fast. In preparation for the feast to end the Holy Month, my mother would take us out shopping for new clothes. Family and friends would visit, laden with treats, toys, and cash gifts known as Eidiya. My father, a tumbler of whisky on the rocks at hand—his first in a month—would carve the roast lamb.

Neither my mother, nor her mother, nor any female member of my family has ever worn a headscarf, or *hijab*. This was a point of pride celebrated as proof of our family's long-established, multigenerational, spirited, and progressive female culture. It is hard to believe today, but the headscarf was rare, especially among younger women. Even more rare was the *niqab*, the full covering of the face. Some Kuwaiti women wore *burqas* (full-body covering), but that was understood as a Kuwaiti national or cultural choice and not a religious Muslim choice.

Unlike Judaism and Christianity, Islam has no confirmation rituals such as baptisms and bar mitzvahs. Any person who utters the *shahada* (proclamation of faith), "I bear witness that there is no god but God, and I bear witness that Muhammad is a messenger of God," is a Muslim. As a first step in my Muslim education, my mother had me memorize Al Fatihah, the most important Muslim prayer, akin to the Lord's Prayer. When I misbehaved, my mother often used Islam to steer me to the straight path. She would quote scripture or traditional Muslim sayings to remind me that God commanded respect for all mothers and that it was forbidden to be undutiful to one's mother. If I sighed in exasperation, which happened often, she reprimanded me with her favorite verse: "And say not to them a word of contempt, nor repel them, but address them in terms of honor. . . . My Lord! bestow upon them Your Mercy even as they cherished me in childhood."[2] At woeful times in her life, my mother would seek the comfort of ritualistic daily prayer more regularly, yet she would not think twice about also asking her good Christian friends to light a candle or two for her at church. Her comfort with other faiths harks back to her Palestinian roots and a time when Islam was not so "Wahhabified." Wahhabism is a sect of Islam named after its founder, Ibn Abd al-Wahhab, who "branded all who disagreed with him as heretics and apostates."[3]

Wahhabism is a fundamentalist, puritanical, and austere religious movement that seeks to purify Islam, rejecting any historical, legal, and theological traditions outside the seventh-century life of the Prophet and his companions. It rejects all esoteric and mystical readings of the Quran, including any idea of saints. In many ways Wahhabism is essentially an aberration from centuries of Muslim theological tradition. However, it has become the most recognizable and dominant modern voice of Islam because it forms the political foundation of the oil-rich Saudi state.

Firm believers in the merits of an education, my parents placed us in the best private school they could find, which in Kuwait at the time happened to be the French lycée, even though neither my brother nor I spoke French. At school I wrote letters to "Cher Papa Noël," or "Dear Father Christmas," and danced the color purple in my school's production of *Joseph and the Amazing Technicolor Dreamcoat.* Maybe because Muslims believe in Mary, the virgin birth of Jesus, and the Jewish prophets before him, my mother never felt a contradiction in the Christmas stockings she hung on our bedposts, nor in the Advent calendar filled with Santa-shaped chocolates that she hung up in the kitchen. Predictably, she baked the best *bûche de Noël,* a traditional Christmas cake in the shape of a log decorated with chocolate shavings, as the dessert to accompany her chestnut-stuffed turkey. We drew the line when it came to roast suckling pig. We were too Muslim to stomach that.

As long as I can remember, I have had the "God gene," and I seemed to come by that naturally; many in my family did too. Under the Ottoman Empire my father's ancestors, the Tabari family, served their community as sheiks (religious leaders), Islamic scholars, and judges. My own spiritual quest started when I was eight. Early indications included a macabre preoccupation with death. I remember fighting off sleep for fear that if I gave in to slumber, I would never wake up. In the backseat of the car I would stare out the window at the vast star-spangled sky and wonder about God. Was he watching over us? Could he hear my thoughts, feel my fears, answer my questions? One moment I was blessed, happy, and bewitched by all the good and plenty of life. Other moments I was anxious, worried about my parents, their health, and our ultimate death. *Will I know you in heaven?* I asked. And *why live and love if we all must die?* I did not believe that I could handle the pain of the permanent separation of death. My mother would use Islam to soothe my fears and negotiate my anxieties. "In the afterlife those who were not as blessed in life will receive their reward and compensation," she would argue, "and it is as natural as birth." God is benevolent and kind, I was told. God is merciful and no matter how bad you think you have been, the measure of an atom of good would tip the scales and erase all the bad. Temptation is how God tests us, she explained. I spent a good part of my childhood convinced that there was an angel sitting on my right shoulder looking out for me, and the devil on my other shoulder trying to lead me astray. And although a number of religion teachers in middle school would paint a more severe, punitive God, I held on to the loving God my mother helped me understand. A God I prayed to every night, grateful for his generous blessings. A God I have physically felt in the flutter of my heart, soaring with elated happiness and in fleeting moments of unbearable beauty: the warmth of a spring sun after a long winter, the perfect kiss under the perfect cherry blossom tree, and the smell and softness of my babies' feet. A God I have appealed to before a big test, prayed compulsively to in panicked fear, and begged for help and forgiveness when I have made my own bad choices and mistakes.

As I matured, I learned to control my fear of death and embrace living in the here and the now. By the time I was twelve my father bought a second home in Virginia, where I spent summers watching reruns of *Bewitched* and *Gilligan's Island.* At sixteen I was already a freshman at Georgetown University, majoring in international politics. A diligent student, I fell in love with our Constitution, the Founding Fathers, and the American dream. At twenty-two, I became a citizen, a proud American: no longer the vulnerable Palestinian whose residency could be revoked on a whim. Growing up, I had felt insecure about my civil rights, as though a loyal citizen of nowhere. I was born in Kuwait, but by age eight had moved to Dubai because of my father's work. I carried the passport of a country I had never visited: Jordan. Rumor had it that the Jordanian passports given to many Palestinian refugees such as my parents were encoded to distinguish them from authentic Jordanians. I remember the pride I felt the day I became an American citizen (and still do every time I travel and stand in the US citizens' airport immigration line). At last I felt secure. I knew that my rights as an individual were preserved and protected, irrefutable and sacred to the Constitution. America's history and its exceptionalism, its guiding light, became my own, my chosen home.

Islam had taken a backseat to more immediate, pressing concerns: graduate degrees, love, marriage, and babies. Sure, I had taken several theology courses at Georgetown. I was religiously literate in a way that allowed me to define the Twelve Shias or elaborate on the story of the disappearing Imams (Islamic leaders). But I had not thought about God and Islam and what they meant to me personally. My life as an American went on, with little thought about my faith.

When the 9/11 attacks occurred, I was caught off guard. Suddenly, Islam was on trial. I was a Muslim in name and upbringing. My husband and I had signed our *kitab* (marriage contract) in 1994 at the Ninety-Sixth Street Mosque in New York City, but we had never been back. Any praying I did was in the solitude of my home to the same loving God my mother had helped me find. In the aftermath of 9/11, now a mother of my own two young children, I was no longer sure that my mother's God still existed, or what exactly it would mean for my children to be both American and Muslim. But I did understand early on that the Islam I was handing down to my American-born children had become more of a burden than a privilege. Even over a decade on, classmates think it is funny to call my son a "terrorist." As a mother, I owed my children explanations. I did not think it fair or responsible of me to ask them to stay true to the faith of their ancestors out of pure loyalty. I had to learn how to empower and shield them, to answer their questions and wipe away the tears. I had some choices to make. I had to figure out why I choose to be a Muslim.

TWO

Accidental Muslims

And revere the wombs that bore you.

—Quran 4:1

ISLAM WAS NOT ON OUR MINDS WHEN MY husband, Sami, and I decided to start a family. Unexplained lower abdominal pains had plagued me all my life, and my OB/GYN was worried that possible endometriosis might complicate my chances of pregnancy. His advice, "Try sooner rather than later," bore unexpected, though successful, results. We worried that our marriage was too young; we had not had a chance to be, to travel, to linger quietly over coffee on lazy Sunday mornings. I did not thrive in pregnancy. My marriage and I suffered from nine months of nausea and heartburn. For a good four months I wiped away excessive saliva, an extreme pregnancy condition that left my inflamed lips raw with blisters and pain. Nausea that woke me up retching in the middle of the night confirmed that it was not "all in my mind." Bags of glucose delivered intravenously for nourishment were often my daily bread.

As my due date approached, the October Jewish holidays were on my mind. I was relieved when early contractions during this time proved to be a false alarm: I wanted my Jewish doctor to be available for this Muslim mom. On the afternoon of November 13, 1995, I held on to Sami in the back of a yellow taxicab, tentative and anxious as we made our way to New York Hospital in Manhattan. I was terrified of the promise of pain, anxious to meet the baby who had kicked and turned all night, and apprehensive about motherhood and its unforgiving demands.

In the birthing room, attached to the monitor, I watched closely, riveted by the fluctuating green jagged line that charted the course of my intensifying contractions. When relief finally arrived in the form of a massive epidural needle, I had no qualms about being numbed. No Christian guilt for me about the pain of labor being a requisite biblical penance for the indiscretions of Eve.

Instead, I held on to my mini Quran, tightening my grip around it, seeking the comfort of its edges as I recited over and over again from a short list of verses memorized all the way back in grade school. That is how I felt most comfortable: the monitor, God, and my doctor by my side. No distracting chitchat or small talk for me. I needed a certain amount of introspective solitude. My body in tune to a divine plan—a mere conduit—I was no longer in command. I could not stop the progress of labor if I wanted to. All I could do was hope that I was up to the task and submit. Finally, when I was asked to push, I was eager to oblige. "Don't forget to pray," my mother had instructed me, "especially near the end, when the head comes down; that's when the heavens are open." With that last push I understood; I felt eternity, an overwhelming physical elation, an uncontainable joy, a connection to the divine.

"She has dimples," were my doctor's first words as Leia loudly made herself heard, "and a full head of straight black hair." In a couple of months she would shed that hair and grow the golden curls that I had seen her wear early on in my pregnancy dreams. The nurses whisked her away and wiped her down; footprints, weight, and length were dutifully noted. Then they brought her back, wrapped in a hospital blanket with a funny pink beanie on her head, and laid her across my breastbone. "Hello, daughter. You know my voice." Or at least that's what *What to Expect When You're Expecting* had led me to believe. I held her tight and prayed for the gift of a lifetime together. I could hardly sleep that night from excitement. The nurses put her by my bed in a clear plastic bassinet with a pink heart attached, announcing, "I am a girl." I could not take my eyes off her. Even when they took her away, her face was seared in my mind's eye so that she was all I could see or feel.

Soon that pink heart registered a name: *Leia*. Many years later, at fifteen, she would question our choice. "Mom, we're studying the Bible in school. Did you know that Leah is the less attractive wife of Jacob?" I hadn't really thought about the Jewish connection or the meaning of her name. I simply liked the way it sounded. In Arabic, Laya means "the green open meadows." It is also the pronoun for "mine," making it doubly appealing to me.

If people thought it was a Jewish name, so be it. That may have even added to its allure. I liked the idea of a name that had cultural relevance and different meanings in different languages and for different people. This was an established, long-standing tradition in the Muslim world. Even Sarah, the biblical banisher of Ishmael, and Moussa, or Moses, have long been popular names in Muslim cultures. Though I preferred the more exotic spelling of "Laya," I acquiesced to her father's desired "French spelling." Even if the hospital nurse did nickname her Princess Leia.

Despite the variety of associations people could infer from her name, there was no imprecision in the hospital paperwork that I filled out identifying us as Muslims. Otherwise, how would New York Hospital's official resident Imam, of whose very existence I was completely unaware, have known to pay mother and daughter an unsolicited visit? I took it as an auspicious omen, and after he had whispered the Muslim declaration of faith into her ear, "I bear witness that there is no god but God, and I bear witness that Muhammad is a messenger of God," I offered him the traditional candied pink almonds decorated with pink ribbons and teddy bears that my mother had carried all the way from Dubai as a gesture of gratitude. With no baptisms or confirmation rituals in our faith, I would have my children repeat the *shahada* after me intermittently in the years to come.

In the following months I became attached to a ritual that was developed with my mother to assuage my loneliness as a newly-wed transport to New York, isolated by solitary academic work. My mother, who lived thousands of miles away, had long been waiting for her first grandchild. Shopping filled the void of our absence and was a tangible way of making us a part of her life, and it was a boon to the local economy. My mother shopped for every possible need her granddaughter could have had, real or imagined. Then she would pack all the gifts, ready for my husband to pick up on his periodic business trips to Dubai and bring home to us in New York. In return I would take pictures of Leia, systematically documenting my mother's efforts to dress my daughter exqui-sitely, diligently describing how lovely everything looked and how many compliments we got at the park. One gift that amused me at the time was a beautiful, elaborate, lace baptism gown. I am still not sure that my mother was aware of the religious provenance of the gown, or that she would even have cared. With no baptism to attend, I dressed Leia up as one would a doll, laid her out on the most formal brocade silk cushion I owned, took the requisite photos, and put her back in her onesie in time for lunch. If you had told me then that I would one day be traveling the country, called upon to speak and answer for Islam, I would have thought it nearly impossible.

If I believed there was anything different or exotic about my newborn, it was that she was American-born. Unlike her parents, she was not naturalized or a resident alien but a true native New Yorker. Islam was an afterthought. When I filled out the hospital paperwork, checking the Muslim box for religion, I was merely entering in a category; that's how my family identified itself. My own faith was quiet, private, and spiritual. I took it for granted. It was neither who I was nor all I was.

I was a lot more than that. I was now first and foremost a mother: the mother of a newborn who was not fond of naps. I promise you she gave them up when she was only three months old. No matter what time I put her down at night, she would still wake up by 4:00 A.M. Only a bottle would calm her down. I did not have the heart to "Ferberize" her, letting her cry it out until she slept through the night.[1] I broke every rule in every how-to baby book. I took it as a sign of her intelligence when she quickly learned to reject all silicone pacifiers in favor of warm milk delivered on demand throughout the night. Desperate, I brought her into our bed, and she soon settled in permanently, a fixture separating Mom from Dad. Like many other mothers, I wondered if I would ever again sleep through the night.

Soon we were four. In bed, I gave my back to Leia the toddler, whose active nocturnal kicking threatened a full and pregnant belly that belied my naturally small frame. Tired of being squeezed out, Leia up and left our bed one night for the independence and comfort of her own. She never looked back, even after her brother claimed the space that had previously belonged to her. At three, she already had an astute mind and a determined will.

A die-hard *Teletubbies* fan, Leia was aching for a purple Tinky Winky, but we held out. This had nothing to do with the conservative religious objections of the time protesting Tinky Winky's alleged sexual orientation. He just happened to be the Teletubby that was missing from her collection. We hoped that his timely purchase would be the bribe, delivered by her newborn brother, that would ease the intrusion of his arrival. This did not prevent Leia, who took suspiciously well to her newborn brother his first week home, from asking in the second week of her baby brother's life, "Does he have to stay here forever? When can we give him back to the hospital?"

It is tradition in the Middle East to name your firstborn son after his paternal grandfather. Young and demure at the time, I made the appropriate, respectful offer to my husband, even though I was rooting for a different name. My father-in-law's name, Yasser, would have burdened our son with troublesome political associations, not to mention the fact that when repeated rapidly it sounds like "Yes sir." I was relieved when my father-in-law graciously relieved us of that traditional duty.

It did not take us long to agree on a new name. We wanted a name that would be relatively easy for English speakers to pronounce and would still resonate with our family's heritage. Taymor, which means "to thrive" in Arabic or "iron" in its original Turkic root, quickly became our choice. In spite of our careful deliberations, Taymor would also grow to question our choice. "Just call me Jack," he would insist when he was only five, after being embarrassed by a sports coach who had a particularly difficult time remembering his name.

I soon gave up hope of ever finishing my PhD. I had completed my coursework but had a lot more writing to do for my thesis. Motherhood consumed me. I could not even read the paper. Even Saddam Hussein's exploits and the crisis in Iraq simply could not compete with my children's many firsts. First words, kisses, and lollipops. First snowman, pink leotard, and light-up sneakers. First Halloween costumes. First collection of seashells. First time down the big slide, all on their own. First bubble-gum balloon and success at snapping fingers. First fevers and the struggles of the medicine dropper. First books. There were many of those: Dr. Seuss's *The Cat in the Hat* and our perennial favorite, *Guess How Much I Love You.* "To the moon and back" is how we still sign off, paraphrasing Big Nutbrown Hare's love for Little Nutbrown Hare.

September 11, 2001, promised to be a beautiful day in New York, with a bright sun and crisp early-fall air. It was also Leia's first official day of kindergarten. After an arduous process, which in New York involved early testing and interviews, Leia was accepted at one of the city's prestigious all-girl schools.

Sami, the proud father, took pictures of her in her pleated, starched-stiff, green plaid uniform, kissed us all good-bye, and left for work. Taymor, a toddler by now, would start a few hours of nursery school in the following weeks. That day he was to stay home. I had asked our babysitter to come in early so I could accompany Leia to school and give her my undivided attention. Her empty oversized backpack held one thing: a tiny mini Quran. I had faithfully packed it, a talisman of hope and protection as we entered a new stage in our relationship, defined by longer school-day separations. As I walked out the door, I could never have imagined that the same Quran I had packed so lovingly would soon be used to wreak the havoc, death, and destruction that were delivered that day. As Leia walked into class, I blew a kiss into her palm to catch and hold on to tightly. I did not know that two jets were about to slam into the World Trade Center, forever entombing in the rubble a father's kisses to his daughter, the girl who sat next to Leia at school, and infinite unknown kisses from mothers to sons to wives to husbands to friends and lovers.

Later on that afternoon we sat huddled around the television, forcing a false calm on the insanity of the day. We were not alone. Two families called and asked if they could join us. One family was Jewish and the other was Christian, both dear and close friends. I did not question it at the time, but now I cannot help but wonder why they wanted to be with us, in our home. Were they looking for answers from Muslims like us? Like it or not, had we unwittingly become representatives of our faith?

I did not know it then, but parenting would never be the same. I would no longer be able to parent without addressing the elephant in the room: Islam. Even if I chose to ignore it, it would not ignore me. Almost a decade following the attack on the World Trade Center, my son was asked by an older boy at school if, as a Muslim, he celebrated 9/11. And that was *before* the uproar over the proposed "Ground Zero Mosque" in New York City.

Most Muslims I know agree that if it was difficult to be a Muslim parent in America just after 9/11, it is now even more challenging. Islam has become a point of departure for American Muslim parents, the subtext and the backdrop against which we are obliged to parent. We have a choice. We can teach our children to reject or distance themselves from the faith. (I have often heard American Muslim children reassure friends that they are not "really religious" or that they do not "really practice Islam" as a way of distancing themselves from Islam's embedded stereotypes.) Or we can teach them to engage and learn about the issues, stereotypes, and challenges that continue to come their way, with the hope that their uncompromising faith in the higher ideals of their identities as Americans and as Muslims will make them empowered agents of change, promising a better future for all.

THREE

The Faith Club,
My Abrahamic Family

Do not argue with the People of the Book unless it is in the politest manner.

—Quran 29:46

MY QUAINT AND PRIVATE ISLAM, WITH ITS FA-
milial rituals and traditions, was being accosted. It had become
public property and, for many, a public enemy. Overnight, every
talking head on television, every pundit, every journalist, had become an expert on all things Muslim. Muslims, especially women,
had to be rescued from Islam. Americans started "learning" that
if Muslims were peaceful, it was in spite of—not because of—
their religion. The terrorists were merely following the Quran,
which commands its followers to kill in its name. Should anyone

harbor hope about alternative theological interpretations derived from specific historical contexts, it was effectively dispelled, as the Quran was described as the absolute word of God, thereby making Islam and Muslims by definition archaic and unreformable. Everyone was talking about the clash of civilizations: the West and its values of enlightenment being threatened by the Muslim barbarians from the East. To sum it up, Islam was violent, punitive, anti-women, anti-freedom, anti-democracy, anti-reform, and anti-progress. Who in their right mind would choose to bring their children up as Muslims?

Here I was: a Muslim by birth, an accidental Muslim, not quite sure if I qualified as a Muslim or if I should ask my American children to remain Muslim only out of a sense of ancestral loyalty. I was desperate, isolated, and equally alienated from the experts who vilified Islam and from those who for the most part spoke for it. I did not know enough to separate fact from fiction. Our family's status as a Muslim family was also open to public debate. Some excused us from all things Muslim because they perceived us to be non-religious and therefore "not Muslim enough." Others believed, as one well-meaning mother who was concerned for our safety sought to reassure me, that "we did not look Muslim." Another mother was equally confident, after learning of the Muslim provenance of my son's name, that we were "not really going to bring him up as a Muslim."

My husband and I, in days of earlier innocence, before Islam became feared as un-American and a national threat to "our way of life," had not discussed our children's religious upbringing. We were both secular Muslims. I, with strong spiritual inclinations, assumed that I would spearhead the effort in the way I had always practiced Islam, according to my terms and family traditions. Sami was happy to defer. With no Muslim community to turn to, no Imam to consult, and no mosque that we attended, I felt stranded, confused, and isolated. The new, post-9/11 world was different from the one that had formed many of my earlier convictions and beliefs. Suddenly, even my assumptions about the guarantees of American citizenship were in jeopardy. Was it all just wishful thinking? What if another "Muslim attack" happened on American soil? Would we end up in camps, interned? Even Sami, who is not prone to anxiety, was anxious.

While I grappled with my own stance on our faith, it was becoming clear that both of my children needed some religious and spiritual guidance. Already, Leia had come home that first term of kindergarten confused by her music teacher, who wanted to know if she celebrated Hanukah or Christmas. Taymor, younger but just as challenging, contrary to expert opinion in the field, understood the permanence of death. He was obsessed: "What happens when you die? Where do you go? How do you know? And will heaven have chocolates, candies, and lollipops?" His pragmatic sister was one day so tired of listening to him go on about the delights of a chocolate-laden heaven that she rolled her eyes and said, "And watch him want to die tomorrow." Clearly, he had inherited his mother's macabre preoccupation with the end of life. He was a child who was wired to need God. I had to help guide him through his blossoming spiritual quest at a time when my spirituality was in a full-blown crisis.

Confused and anxious, I hit the books. I spent hours seeking comfort in the solitude of my home, searching for answers. I picked up the Quran and read it for the first time. I read Karen Armstrong, Michael Gilsenan, Bruce Feiler. I surfed the Internet. It did not take me long to connect with what I believe to be the universal truths within Islam, truths that had never been highlighted in many years of compulsory religion classes required by my grade school. It was as if Islam were being revealed to me for the first time. I was appreciating its message in a whole new light. Salutations of peace offered to Abraham and his descendants, including Moses, Jesus, and Muhammad, at the end of Muslim ritualistic prayers, performed five times a day, took my breath away with their interfaith message of love. I was incredulous when I read in Muslim canonic law that "he who believes all that he is bound to believe, except that he says, 'I do not know whether Moses and Jesus (Peace be upon them) do or do not belong to the Messengers,' is an infidel."[1] I knew that I could not believe in a God who was a discriminator at heart or a God who would choose or who would leave a people behind. I was delighted to find out that Islam reveres religious diversity:

We have sent down the Torah, which contains guidance and light . . . later, we sent Jesus, son of Mary, confirming the Torah, which has been sent down before him, and gave him the Gospel containing guidance and light. Unto you, O Muhammad, We have revealed the book [Quran] with truth. It confirms the scriptures, which came before it. Unto every one of you we have appointed a different law. And if God had willed, he could surely have made you all one single community professing one faith.[2]

Islam, in contrast to what I was hearing in the media, was modern in sensibility, respectful of diversity. It did not seek to deny the truths that came before it; rather, it came to renew and confirm them. One story in particular stood out, which set my heart racing with excitement. It is the vision of the Prophet in his night-flight journey in which he is transported to Jerusalem and ascends the heavens to the threshold of the kingdom of God:

On a night when Muhammad could not fall asleep, he made his way to the Ka'aba, Mecca's holiest shrine, where he prayed and soon found peaceful sleep. No sooner had he surrendered to slumber than he was awakened, startled by the angel Gabriel, who appeared before him holding a golden goblet and leading a dazzling white, winged horse. "Drink," said Gabriel as he held the cup to Muhammad's lips. Muhammad drank from the golden goblet of wisdom and faith.

Gabriel beckoned Muhammad to mount Baraq, a celestial horse that had been ridden to the heavens by Abraham, Moses, and Jesus before him. Muhammad climbed onto

Baraq's back, and in only a few strides they flew all the way to Jerusalem, to the farthest mosque. Muhammad tied Baraq to the hitching post used by God's prophets before him. A ladder of silver and gold embedded with pearls miraculously appeared, and Muhammad and Gabriel climbed the ladder into the heavens.

They rose as the gates of heaven were opened. In the first heaven, Muhammad was received and welcomed by Adam, the first man God placed on earth. Gabriel then led him to the higher heavens, where he met Abraham, Moses, Jesus, John the Baptist, Joseph, and Mary, who welcomed him as a righteous man, a brother, and a fellow prophet. Finally, Gabriel took Muhammad even higher until they reached the lote tree, the boundary of the throne of God. The sweet-smelling tree, whose leaves were as big as elephant ears, marked the limit of human knowledge. By the tree, two milky white rivers ran with floating vessels of gold and silver. Along the banks of these two rivers, Muhammad saw silken tents, sparkling with iridescent jewels and gems of pearls and sapphires. Enchanting green birds flew overhead, and when Muhammad bent down to taste the river water, it was sweeter than honey. He looked up, and there were seventy thousand angels at prayer.[3]

At the end of the vision, Muhammad, Moses, and Jesus descend and engage in interfaith communal prayers by the Temple

Mount in Jerusalem. *Why weren't Muslims sharing this story with the rest of the world?* I wondered. In my hour of frustration and need I felt the hand of divine intervention. It was as if the heavens were steering me.

I could not contain my excitement. I wanted the world to know. I could not walk away. As a Muslim, it became my religious duty to speak up and to share, to teach my children to speak up, to counter the voices of extremism, violence, and fear. Wouldn't it be wonderful if I could reach out to a Christian mother and a Jewish mother with the idea of doing a project that would help highlight the commonalities among the three faiths? I was actively on the lookout when I met Suzanne Oliver at our daughters' school bus stop. I knew right there and then that I had found my spiritual partner from the gleam in her eyes as I described my interest in possibly writing a children's book about the Abrahamic faiths. She would later confess that she went to work immediately on finding a Jewish mother for our group, as a way of securing her spot. Priscilla Warner was home when she received the call from Suzanne, who had managed to get her number from a friend at nursery school who thought Priscilla might be a good fit for our proposed project. Priscilla, a Jewish mother and a writer, was curious enough to agree to meet. At our first meeting we were strangers to one another, but even then the air felt charged with promise and spiritual adventure. As we met for the first time in my apartment over tea and biscuits, the conversation overflowed. Truth be told, it did not take long for our commonalities to give way to our differences. A few meetings on and we had outright conflict; but as any mother would, we persevered, for there was a lot at stake: the very security and future of our children. Instead of calling it quits, we committed to the three of us meeting regularly, at least once a week. We became a spiritual cocoon where no question was deemed inappropriate or politically incorrect. We started calling ourselves "The Faith Club," although some have dubbed us more fight club than faith club. Over four years we met weekly, and we never shied away from asking the tough questions. We pushed ourselves outside our comfort zones. We were determined not to be inhibited by political correctness; we wanted instead to enlighten our thoughts. The three of us emerged more anchored in our own faiths, empowered by our spiritual growth and friends for life. The Faith Club rescued me from spiritual isolation; it became my spiritual anchor: my temple, my church, and my mosque, right there in my living room.

Even traditions that I had growing up, which I had always assumed cultural or idiosyncratic to my family, took on newly discovered religious and spiritual significance. Holiday rituals I have long enjoyed, such as Christmas caroling and holiday cards, acquired spiritual undertones that were very much rooted in Islam. Christmas was not just cultural or commercial anymore. When I assured Leia and Taymor that, contrary to their friends' insistence, Santa could visit Muslim children, I did not feel theologically absurd. Muslims believe in the birth of Jesus, who is believed to be one of twenty-five prophets we are asked to revere. This line of prophets begins in the Old Testament and runs through the New Testament and is a precursor to the Prophet Muhammad. Muslims do not believe Jesus to be either the Son of God or God, nor do we believe in the Holy Trinity. But if Christmas is about celebrating the birth of Jesus, then I do not see why as Muslims who believe in the Quran—which has an entire chapter dedicated to Mary, a woman described as "chosen above the women of all nations to deliver the promised Messiah, Jesus"[4]—we cannot enjoy some Christmas cheer. Just in case my children missed the point, I took out a copy of the Quran and read from it: "Remember when the angels said, 'O Mary, God gives you good news of a word from him, whose name is the Messiah Jesus, son of Mary, revered in this world and the Hereafter. . . . He will speak to the people from his cradle and as man, and he is of the righteous,' she said, 'My Lord, how can I have a child when no mortal has touched me?'"[5]

I was no longer an accidental Muslim. The Faith Club had helped me find my footing within the extended Judeo-Christian tradition; in my mind it became the Judeo-Christian-Muslim tradition. I truly felt empowered, a more confident, affirmed Muslim who had ownership of her religion. I no longer felt alone. I had connected with a progressive American Muslim community. I had reached a new spiritual awareness, harnessed and propelled by my love and concern for my children. I had even found my Imam. He gave my growing commitment and understanding of Islam the official stamp of approval that I craved. I felt that the Faith Club had made me a better mother. Honestly, I do not know how

I would have dealt with many of the questions and issues my children brought home in those early years without it. When I visited Leia's class, I saw a picture she had drawn for a class project in which she was asked to complete the phrase, "It's okay when . . ." She had drawn herself separate and apart from two other girls holding hands. Her completed phrase read, "It's okay to be Muslim. It makes me feel weird when I am the only Muslim and everyone around me is either Christian or Jewish." I was sad to see how Leia perceived herself and worried about the negative effects of her feelings of emotional and religious isolation. The Faith Club had helped me find my voice as a Muslim; now I needed to help my seven-year-old daughter find hers. Together we prepared a presentation for her class. She asked her class a number of questions, which I hoped would dispel some of the stereotypes: "Do all Muslim girls wear a headscarf? No, it's a choice." "Do Muslims believe in God or Allah?" she asked her classmates. "God, because Allah is just the Arabic word for God, like Dios is God in Spanish. Muslims believe that they worship the same God as the Jews and the Christians," she explained.

The publication of *The Faith Club* in 2006 far exceeded any expectations I had when I was so desperate to connect with my fellow Americans. I toured the United States, traversing its vast landscape from extreme north to south and east to west, an intrepid candidate campaigning for Islam. Long gone were my days of alienation and angst. America had embraced me; it had become an extended Faith Club. We were embraced in dozens of communities by churches, temples, mosques, seminaries, and interfaith organizations full of earnest men and women eager to learn and grow and talk. As a mother, it was particularly rewarding to be received by audiences eager to hear what I had to say, especially since those days my children were all too happy to ignore me. I once was asked by a Muslim audience member, "Aren't you tired of explaining yourself?" On the contrary: every time I am asked to speak, I feel it is a gift, an opportunity to engage, to clarify and speak up against fears and misconceptions.

Many Americans do not have the opportunity to meet a Muslim in person, to put a human face on a religion they know only through the latest headline news. Their fears are real. Islam at best is judged as foreign to American values and at worst as a risk to our security. It is no wonder that statistics confirm that so many Americans worry about having a Muslim as a neighbor. In fact, 39 percent of Americans favor requiring Muslims, including American Muslims, to carry special identification. A staggering 41 percent would be uncomfortable if a teacher at the elementary school in their community were Muslim.[6] No wonder a grandmother in Kansas who was close to tears beseeched me to reassure her: "Are you sure that all Muslims are not out to get us? Will my grandchildren be safe?" In spite of my fear of flying, I felt blessed every time I boarded a plane. Whatever maternal guilt I had about my intermittent absences from home I assuaged with deeply held convictions about our need as Americans to engage and converse. My fortitude to board yet another plane is the fortitude of any mother concerned for her children. America's vastness, its mountains, lakes, and neatly gridded square fields inspired and overwhelmed me; it also punctuated the smallness of my family and made me worry for their future. I hoped when I was no longer around, my two children in turn would also be embraced; that they would find their own meaningful, secure, American Muslim niche. For now, all I could do was help pave the way.

FOUR

A Crisis of Faith

Sticks and Stones Can Hurt My Bones, but God Should Not Hurt Me

To whom should we show the most kindness? Your mother, then your mother, then your mother, and then your father.

—The Prophet Muhammad[1]

"WHERE ARE THE MODERATE MUSLIMS?" WAS the question most frequently asked of me during my speaking engagements. Honestly, I was quite suspicious of the question and a little dismissive. "Look around you," I would say. "There are 1.6 billion moderate Muslims going about living average, un-newsworthy lives."[2] When a Muslim mother prepares two fried eggs and sends her children to school, it does not make our six o'clock news. Sometimes I wondered if the question was a polite way of masking my audience's fears that as a Muslim who seemed a lot like them, I was the exception and not the norm. This nagging suspicion was reinforced when people asked if "they can clone me." Frustrated, I assured them that I was but one of many, an average and typical Muslim in America, one of thousands who are serving in our armed forces, healing patients as doctors and nurses, and teaching children in our schools. For those who needed more examples, I referenced numerous Muslim petitions and organizations that have actively distanced themselves from the violence and politics of radical Islam. I felt equipped to handle the question and confident of my answers.

Until one warm fall morning. After early morning errands, I like to settle in with a cup of coffee and listen to the news on NPR, reported in soothing British tones by the BBC News service, tones that transport me back to my childhood and my grandfather's prized bedside transistor radio. This morning, those tones could do little to temper my rage as I listened to gruesome details of the unfolding scene. The reporter recounted that a young girl named Aisha had naively sought the help of a Somali Sharia (Islamic law) court to report her rape and ended up being charged with adultery. Her punishment came swiftly. She was buried alive and stoned to death as she cried and pleaded for help. Armed men prevented the watching crowd from helping. On that day, thirteen-year-old Aisha, the very same age as my daughter, and whose name in tragic irony means "she lives," was murdered in the name of "Muslim justice." I sat alone at my kitchen table and wept. And I finally asked myself the same questions that had been asked of me across America: *Where are the moderates?* and *What are they saying and doing?*

That morning marked the beginning of a renewed and acute crisis of faith. All at once, these questions that had seemed banal and naive resonated with urgency, as if I were hearing them for the first time with a new set of ears. In the course of my interfaith discussions in the Faith Club I had questioned Christianity and Judaism, pressed Suzanne and Priscilla to answer my questions, and held them accountable for their religions. Aisha's stoning compelled me to turn the lens inward and hold the mirror up to myself and to my fellow Muslims. Whereas before I could have rationalized Aisha's murder as an aberration committed by an anarchic failed state, with no immediate relevance or threat to 1.6 billion Muslims, now—spiritually and emotionally—I needed more. Aisha's short, tragic life took on much-needed urgency. She was denied her life, denied the chance to potentially be a mother to her own children. I wanted my children to feel her pain, to bring her unimaginable death into our home, not to be lulled by the distance that separates us. We owe her that much.

Truth be told, I was suffering from a full-blown, severe case of Muslim fatigue. Faith is never static, and if it is to remain vibrant and relevant, it must continue to push boundaries and actively seek growth. When I was on the road, I was unwittingly transformed by my audience's fear, questions, and hesitations. Alone at home, these became my own. Now I wondered whether I truly believed the comforting reassurances of shared humanity and universal values that my audiences were so eager to receive. I questioned the credibility of my own words. Was the gap between the ideals of Islam that I so desperately hung on to and the Islam that is practiced on the ground too big to bridge?

My discomfort grew with every dose of "Muslim misgiving" delivered to my door with depressing frequency. Every paper I picked up, every television news report I turned on, every airwave I listened to, tore at my confidence, insulted my spirituality, and threatened to embarrass my family. The fault line between my children's identities as Americans and their identities as Muslims was widening, threatening to erupt into uninhabitable space. Atrocities carried out in the name of Islam demanded that I reexamine the issues if I were to sustain my faith. These included stories of a British teacher in Sudan criminalized for allowing her six- and seven-year-old Muslim students to name a teddy bear Muhammad, a Saudi senior citizen threatened with lashes for the crime of being alone with a young delivery man, and potential lashings for the crime of drinking beer in Malaysia or wearing pants in Sudan. The list goes on and on, a list so bizarre that it would have been laughable if it were not true and tragic. I was furious, ashamed, and frustrated for my children, who would be forced to not only face the challenges of growing up, but also have the added complication of having to define their religious identity in defiance and in negation of these embarrassing and alarming episodes carried out in the name of their religion. I realized that I needed answers to the issues that will taunt and challenge my children's faith and their identities as Americans and as Muslims. I needed absolute and unequivocal Muslim positions: ones that abandoned stoning to a less savory historical past and denied its possibility of ever being a part of our present or our future.

I was in search of an Islam of the twenty-first century—one sustained by values that are relevant to our present and not invested in a revered seventh-century utopian ideal. I needed to empower my children against Muslim clerics who have appointed themselves God's only legitimate intermediaries on earth, who act as if to question them is to question God. I cannot let my children be intimidated by clerics who peddle seventh-century absolute orthodoxy as the only true Islam. As American Muslims, they need to recognize and voice the difference between culture and theology and not be shut down by those who confuse the two. To carry with conviction their identities as American Muslims, they need to hold both America and Islam accountable to the promises of their ideals.

I want them to be Muslims and Americans who speak up. Patient but resolute with those who insist that only extreme readings of Islam are authentic, never settling on being treated as lesser Americans. As Muslims, they need to demand a zero-tolerance policy from Muslims who insist that stoning, floggings, and amputations are elemental to being Muslim. Muslims, I remind them, did not invent stoning. Just as Jews do not defend the practice as a core value of their Jewish identity, neither should Muslims. We need to demand the eradication of outdated, inhumane, severe corporal punishments from the Muslim penal code without any conditions or qualifications.

I am asking a lot of my children because with knowledge comes freedom, and with freedom comes duty. Thankfully, my children and I are not alone. We are fortified by Muslim scholars and thinkers who refuse to be intimidated. They vehemently reject these severe and cruel punishments as being anachronistic and offensive to our twenty-first-century sensibilities. They have done a tremendous amount of work to support the position that there is no room for stoning, amputations, and floggings in an Islam of the twenty-first century. They have divorced Islam from these punishments, proving that they do not embody or define the ideal or true Islam. On the contrary, Dr. Nasr Abu Zayd, an Egyptian scholar who received death threats and was charged with apostasy by the Egyptian courts—which then demanded that his Muslim wife divorce him—asserts: "Contemporary society has every right—even an obligation—to institute more humane punishments for crimes."[3] The forms of punishment mentioned in the Quran are but a historical expression of punishment carried out by a specific society, in a specific time and place, not a divine directive. Dr. Abu Zayd believes that the Quran took a particular shape so that people in seventh-century Arabia would "get it." He explains, "If anything spoken about in the Qu'ran has a precedent in pre-Islamic tradition—whether Jewish, Roman, or anything else—we need to understand that its being mentioned in the Qu'ran does not automatically make it Qur'anic and therefore binding on Muslims." Lastly, he asserts, "People who think that everything mentioned in the Qu'ran is binding, should be obeyed, and followed literally, are going against God's word."[4]

Our identities as American Muslims are built on shifting sands, perpetually vulnerable to events that are completely out of our control. As Americans we are judged, stereotyped, pitied, or feared in relation to the latest headline news or calamitous event. As Muslims, we are at the mercy of an Islam that is in flux, accommodating social and political upheavals continents away. As American Muslims, we are challenged at the most unexpected moments and in the most unanticipated ways by the resulting stereotypes and prejudices that seep into our lives: in history books, on posters plastered to buses, at book clubs, or in the anxiety of a ten-year-old boy who worries that his Muslim name could exclude him from the honor of being flag-bearer at his school's weekly Friday assembly. There are days when I second-guess my choices—when boys have spent the hour in study hall at school looking up racist Muslim jokes, which are normally shrugged off by my composed son, but hit home in the middle of an emotionally vulnerable night. "Why can't I be like everyone else?" he moans through sincere but rare tears. "But you are." In these moments, my efforts to comfort him are plagued by a well-earned adult cynicism, which I try to conceal. Yet, the earnest American in me, confirmed and affirmed on the road, in hundreds of communities across America, endures: it continues to believe in the possibility of being "like everybody else": American, Muslim, and proud.

Too often, the choice in the West is cast as if it were a battle between Islam and secular Muslims, a choice that many Muslims appear to confirm when they describe themselves as secular Muslims or non-religious Muslims. I do not feel that this is a wise choice. We must give our children other options. To abandon or to call oneself not-quite Muslim is not just semantics. It has real and important consequences. It denies the possibility of the natural and necessary diversity that exists and has always existed within Islam. I remind my children not to be intimidated by Muslims or non-Muslims who, for different reasons, are eager to dismiss them as untrue or inauthentic Muslims because they do not fit into their preconceived ideas of what it is to be a Muslim. I tell them that at the end of the day, only God is the judge of our faith. To shrink from Islam or to qualify our Muslim identity is to abandon our religion in its time of need. For all the stereotypes and challenges, for all the misconceptions and fear, I still expect my children to carry the truth of their faith with conviction and pride, to patiently serve as Americans and as Muslims. It takes courage and fortitude to navigate childhood and young adulthood in defiance of those who are too eager to label you or to dismiss you as qualifying for neither or as both. As a mother, I can only hope that those challenges will one day empower my children and make them wiser adults, for as Rumi, the famous Muslim mystic and poet, reminded us, "Burdens are the foundations of ease, and bitter things the forerunners of pleasure."[5]

Many friends have asked me, as I have sometimes wondered myself, why I continue to remain Muslim in spite of my frustrations. The reasons are many, but perhaps the most important is that I remain a Muslim to some degree *because* of my frustrations. I am unwilling to concede defeat. Priscilla and Suzanne, my Jewish and Christian Faith Club companions, are on their own spiritual journeys. These days, Priscilla is more comfortable meditating in Buddhist temples than in Jewish ones, and Suzanne is in the process of deconstructing her faith as she pursues her studies at a theological seminary. I, on the other hand, remain focused on what it means for my family and me to be American and Muslim today. I recently was sent a copy of the book *The Bread of Angels*, in which a priest reflects on being a Christian in the Middle East and writes:

> When you love someone else, you appreciate his way of sitting, acting, drinking, you hope his hopes, you excuse his difficulties, and you recognize his gifts. Love . . . is never abstract. It is always searching for a body. . . . If Muslims must suffer because of their own bad clerics, the tragedy of fundamentalism and the growing stigma against Islam worldwide, then I will not allow them to suffer alone.[6]

I am a daughter of Islam. I have loved its stories, poetry, and people my whole life. I have loved its heroes and heroines. I have loved its prayer beads in the hands of my father and my grandfather before him. I have loved its sights, smells, and sounds; its domes, minarets, and prayers; its art, architecture, mosaics, and ceramics. To have loved is to owe. It is to stand by it in its hour of need. I know no other way.

FIVE

Food for Thought

Show gratitude to Me and to thy parents; to Me is the final goal.

—Quran 31:14

"WHO WROTE THE QURAN?" MY HUSBAND grinned challengingly at me as he handed over the article written under that eye-popping headline one very cold Sunday morning. Just in case the children had missed the point, he added, "I found the perfect article for Mommy." Mommy, notwithstanding her most recent crisis of faith, was still officially this family's resident Muslim expert.

It was a typical Sunday morning in our home. Freed from the myriad of chores and activities, I like to listen to Jack Johnson's "Banana Pancakes" as I prepare a traditional Middle Eastern breakfast, or as my son Taymor protests, "Muslim food." I grill some *halloumi* cheese (salty white sheep's milk), dice a box of cherry tomatoes and some scallions, then mix in a little lemon juice, olive oil, and mint. I prepare an improvised, homemade version of *manaeesh:* pita bread topped with *zaatar,* a middle eastern blend of herbs and spices mixed with sesame seeds and served with olive oil. I like to think of it as our sacred family ritual. We first go around the table, each of us taking turns, as we offer a prayer of thanks for a particular moment or memory of the week. No "thanks" is ever deemed too trivial. Over the years we have run the gamut from "Thank you God that I no longer have that pimple on my face" to the more manipulative "Thank you for Mommy who may still get us a dog one day." Next, my husband, Sami, and I pick out articles of interest from the Sunday papers for the family to read. The children are reluctant participants, so we are constantly scouring the paper for possible enticing articles. On that particular Sunday, I worried that Sami's triumph would prove to be my final defeat: a defeat I had managed to carefully avoid so far in my travels for the Faith Club because the question I feared the most had thankfully never been asked.

Lately, this question had been encroaching on my life, promising unchecked spiritual havoc. It weighed me down as I watched a news segment in which Keith Ellison, the first Muslim elected to Congress, debated Ayaan Hirsi Ali, a fervent critic of Islam. I watched, feeling dejected, as Ayaan used my "red herring" issue: the question of the literal divinity of the word of God in the Quran, to condemn Islam as an archaic religion, by definition impossible to reform. She delivered her final judgment with piercing certainty. She argued that since Muslims believe the Quran to be the literal and divine word of God, the only way forward is for Muslims to condemn their prophet as a lackluster model of violence and for the Quran to have its problematic verses "slashed with a razor." Offended, but uncertain of the truth, I turned the television set off. I was not ready to battle the issue.

My respite was short-lived. My daughter, Leia, brought it home from school soon thereafter. She explained how they were studying the Bible as literature for English class. "God is really angry and vengeful sometimes. And why would Sarah encourage Abraham to take a new wife just because she can't have children?" she asked while sharing her own religious verdict. "Mommy, I know some girls believe that the Bible is the exact word of God. That doesn't make sense to me. Is that okay?" "Sure," I replied. I have to confess, I gave myself a parental pass. I did not point out to her that many Christians were free to believe that the Bible was not the literal and divine word of God. That Christians could do so without feeling intimidated or that they no longer qualified as Christians. I was not sure that this opinion was possible for Muslims. I knew that the literal divinity of the Quran was most certainly a radioactive topic: taboo and off-limits. A tinderbox that should be labeled: "Open at your own risk, explosive reaction guaranteed." Not only did I fear that there was no room for flexibility on the issue, but I knew that I could be labeled a heretic. Was that not the most basic tenet of the faith? The literal divinity of the word of God in the Quran?

What should I tell Leia? That she might as well not call herself a Muslim?

The literal divinity of the word of God in the Quran is a question that I have skirted all my life and have yet to figure out. To be sure, there was a lot at stake. At best, Muslims would find the very question quite offensive. At worst, I would be labeled a heretic, and the violent might use it as an excuse for violence. To be fair, the divinity of the Quran for Muslims is not equivalent to the divinity of the Bible; it is more akin to the divinity of Jesus for Christians. For many, it is the pivotal belief that inoculates members into the faith. It is the benchmark used to define who is and who is not a believer.

Compared to Jesus, Muhammad pales as a miracle worker. He was not walking on water, healing the sick, or turning water into wine. His only miracle is the most important of miracles: the miracle of the Quran. Words whose divine beauty and inimitable poetry are said to have made war-hardened warriors cry and kneel in submission to God. To this day, artistic, elaborate calligraphies of its verses adorn most Muslim homes. Its beauty is celebrated through exquisite, measured, soulful recitations. Its words are a portal to the divine. They are the Muslim Eucharist, transporting the believer from the temporal to the celestial. I should know. I am moved to tears when I allow myself to be carried away by the Quran's hypnotic, measured rhythms.

Those measured rhythms have also been a great source of anxiety for me for different reasons at different stages of my life. As a pigtailed eight-year-old I wondered: *If God was the God of all people, why had he chosen to speak only Arabic? Could God speak other languages?* Such curiosity did not earn me scholarly rewards. In middle school I lived in terror of my religion teacher, who had sternly planted the "fear of God" in me, lest a fellow student or I ever mispronounce or forget a verse in our oral recitations. Such infractions, we were told, no matter whether they were intended or not, were a direct insult to God, whose very words we were corrupting.

When I was a young adult, the Quran was used to censor my doubts, inhibit my questioning, and curtail my curiosity. When others quoted the Quran to justify violence, misogyny, or an injustice, if I dared argue, all they had to do was say, "But it is in the Quran." That was code for, "Do you really want to go up against God?" I for one did not. That fear was effectively harnessed. So, though I secretly wondered if Muslims had virtually replaced the divinity of Jesus with the divinity of the Quran, I never voiced it. I really was not looking to offend. When Muslims questioned the purity of Christian monotheism because of the divinity of Jesus, I had to bite my tongue not to draw a parallel between that and the divinity of the Quran. In my mind, the Quran for many Muslims had become God; to worship God was to worship the Quran. But such thoughts were carefully stored away for fear of insulting, a fear that is so deeply embedded in Muslims that it has my mother pleading with me even today "not to go there."

For the most part, my relationship with the Quran became symbolic, a talismanic verse worn around my neck or kept in my purse for protection. Even as I toured the country as the Muslim member of the Faith Club, I still had not figured out whether there was room for people like my daughter and me within Islam. Could there be more to being a Muslim than a bedrock belief in the literal divinity of the word of God? I was about to find out.

I warmed my hands around my coffee mug, braced myself for the worst, and with the trepidation of a person who had so far managed to preserve her faith but was about to lose that privilege, I began to read Sami's chosen article. Little did I know that I was about to meet a Muslim hero.

Abdolkarim Soroush, an Iranian theological reformer, was initially appointed by Ayatollah Khomeini to "Islamicize" Iran's universities, only to eventually turn against the theocratic state. The price of his dissent was beatings and assassination attempts. The crime of this daring and audacious thinker? He challenged the most sensitive of Muslim issues: the divine origin of the Quran. For those of us who have wondered whether we could be Muslims without believing in the literal divinity of the Quran, Soroush offers an alternative view. He believes that the Quran was a "prophetic experience."[1] He describes Muhammad as being "at the same time the receiver and the producer of the Quran, or if you will, the subject and the object of the revelation."[2] Or more poetically, he was "like a bee who produces honey itself, even though the mechanism for making honey is placed in him by God."[3] The Quran exalts the healing power of honey; I did not know that honey could heal my faith. I paused, trying to absorb the enormity of his words.

He continued, this time leaving the reader no room to doubt his intent, "When you read the Quran, you have to feel like a human being is speaking to you. The words, images, rules and regulations are coming from a human mind. This mind, of course, is special in the sense that it is imbued with divinity and inspired by God."[4] This was huge. I carefully clipped the article. Read and reread it. It was my moment of Muslim reckoning and rebirth. I was ready to receive this holy honey. Islam had not abandoned me; I was not to be forsaken. A sense of relief swept over me. Even joy.

I became obsessed with Soroush. He is one of a growing number of brave progressive Muslims whose work will no doubt serve as the pillars of an Islam of the twenty-first century. An Islam that I could embrace and celebrate. An Islam that is pluralistic, diverse, and democratic. I explained to our children how critics would have loved to dismiss Soroush's work as "Western" or a "foreign import" to Islam. This is because in their hands, Islam is one more tool in the battle of the "politics of identity." Their Islam is all about the rejection of all things Western, a position supported by Samuel Huntington and his "clash of civilizations" theory.[5] That position is completely absurd, for clearly Islam has no nationality, no one country or flag demanding overarching loyalty. "Don't let anyone tell you that you can't be both," I added, "but the best part of Soroush's work is that it is completely based on Islam's own rich tradition of diversity."

Soroush describes himself as an heir to the ninth-century Muslim theological school known as the Mu'tazalites. The

Mu'tazalites believed that the Quran was created and separate from God, and therefore not literally divine. Soroush believes that the Mu'tazalite past holds the key to the future because the Mu'tazalites have shown us that not all issues have to be justified or resolved using religious texts. Sometimes you need to resort to your own reason; we're being told not by non-Muslims, liberals, or secularists, but by our own forefathers. Today, Soroush is just one example of the inspiring work that courageous Muslims are doing. Their task is big and daunting, often fraught with personal dangers and risks.

Progressive Muslims share one common fundamental belief: the need for Muslims to understand the Quran in the context and the culture of its time. This is how the Quran can fulfill its promise to Muslims as a book for all ages and places and a template for social justice. I explained to our children how Islam has a rich tradition of rationalism. Ironically, it is Muslim rationalist thinkers and philosophers, such as Abd al-Jabbar, Ibn Rushd (Averroes), Ibn Sina (Avicenna), Jalal al-Din al-Suyuti, and Wasil Ibn Ata, to name a few, who have historically been credited with planting the seeds of the European Renaissance and the age of Enlightenment. Today, Muslims have abandoned them in favor of the shackles of intellectual tyranny and the confinement of absolute conformity and unquestioning certainty.

"Do you think most Muslims have heard of Soroush? Or the Mu'tazalites, for that matter?" I asked my father somewhat rhetorically, to emphasize my point, as I shared with him the woes of my latest Muslim frustration. "Why did it take the *New York Times* for us to hear of his work?" I added for good measure, "I find it baffling and insulting how little most Muslims know of their own history, and I don't believe that this ignorance is accidental." Muslim children should be learning about Islam's rich history of intellectual diversity. In Saudi Arabia, it is against the law to teach Muslims about Islam's diverse theological traditions. Imams can be trained in, and children are allowed to study, Islam only from the perspective of Wahhabis. Because the Saudis spend millions of petrodollars promoting their take on Islam by building schools and mosques and training Imams worldwide, the effects of such a policy are global. As parents, we need to demand that our children are taught the truth about the history of their faith, not an edited, politically motivated falsity. To empower our children as Muslims, we need them to have real knowledge, which will help them reclaim their religion as a religion of the twenty-first century.

That Sunday as we sat around the kitchen table, I felt nourished and blessed by the love of my family, and I thanked God. A God who cannot be confined between the covers of a book. An intangible God. An uncontainable God. A transcendent God, larger and bigger than the boundaries of our human bodies and minds. A God that I recognized in the work of a young Muslim artist, Farah Behbehani. Her book, *The Conference of the Birds*, inspired and named after Farid ud-Din Attar's twelfth-century Sufi allegorical poem, sits on my coffee table, and I pick it up from time to time. In my favorite silkscreen, "The Seven Valleys of the Way," she begins our journey with the literal, pictorial, and precise, calligraphies of the seven emotions of the birds on their final flight to God: *athiqah* (confidence), *salam* (peace), *hurriya* (freedom), *amal* (hope), *iman* (faith), *hubb* (love), and *farah* (happiness). She then feeds these precise images to a computer program to deconstruct and abstract. My eyes follow the resulting fluttering, suspended forms as they beckon me to journey on. Fluid dots, circular paths, with no beginning or end: just how I imagine God.

SIX

In God We Trust

An American Muslim Knight

There are as many ways to God as there are human souls. (God says) "I do not fit into My heaven and My earth, but I fit into the heart of My believing servant."

—The Prophet Muhammad[1]

"IS THERE SOMETHING WRONG WITH BEING A Muslim in this country?" Colin Powell asked after seeing a photo essay about fallen soldiers that included a picture of a Muslim mother mourning over her son's headstone, which bore the symbols of his faith: a crescent and a star. "The answer is no," he answered. "That's not American." He continued, "Is there something wrong with a seven-year-old Muslim-American kid believing he or she could be president? Yet, I have heard senior members of my own party drop the suggestion, 'He's a Muslim and he might be associated with terrorists.' This is not the way we should be doing it in America."[2] To many—half the country—Powell is wrong. Not only is there something wrong with being a Muslim in this country, but in some circles it is even considered patriotic to be actively anti-Muslim. Four years into his presidency, President Obama was still believed to secretly be an "avowed Muslim," as one woman described him at a Rick Santorum political rally where the politician chose not to correct her. The woman can certainly be forgiven for her convictions, especially since religious leaders such as the Reverend Franklin Graham believe that "Islam has gotten a free pass under Obama" because Muslims see him as a "son of Islam."[3]

When I hear how a Republican American Muslim activist who sought membership in the South Florida Republican Executive Committee was heckled as a terrorist and denied a seat by an overwhelming vote of 158 to 11, I cannot help but feel profound anxiety about my children's futures.[4] Members of the committee rejected his membership because they believed that he was un-American and that his Islam was incompatible with the US Constitution. Bringing up well-adjusted, confident children in this political climate can be a daunting and emotionally taxing task. Challenges often come our way from unforeseen and unpredictable circumstances. In middle school, Leia was studying the Middle Ages when the teacher explained how in those days religious conversion was not as common as it is today, and then he chuckled as he delivered his punch line: "Not that anyone would want to convert to Islam, even today."

Even television viewing can prove to be a perilous act. As a rule we try to steer clear of Fox's more inflammatory shows, such as *Hannity and Friends,* but recently even Jon Stewart on Comedy Central unexpectedly ruffled Taymor. At the time, there was a controversy around some of the fervent opposition to the reelection of a Jewish candidate from Texas. The person being interviewed denied that religion had any relevance. However, when asked if he would feel differently had it been a Muslim candidate, he did not hesitate. He confirmed that he would be suspicious of a Muslim candidate and would worry about the candidate's loyalty to the Constitution. Unfortunately, Taymor heard the clip, and as hard as he tried to hold his emotions in check, a flood of tears came rushing down his cheeks.

Taymor's sensitivity was heightened by what had been happening at school. Apparently, a boy in class had been calling Taymor a terrorist, and a number of jokes ensued about hidden caches of weapons at home, which had a group of boys laughing and eager to pursue the joke regularly. It had started early in the school year, and although it was now late winter, the teasing was not abating. He had chosen not to tell us because he thought he could just laugh it off. "Everyone gets teased, Mom; I was hoping that if I didn't make a fuss of it, they would get bored and stop." When I confided in another mother, she was surprised that I did not want to notify the school. "I would rather he find his own voice," I explained. I am very conscious that inevitably my children will, at various stages of their lives, be exposed to situations that will grate at their identity. Teachers and school will not be there to shield them for life. They have to learn how to address these issues independently and in a way that will heal and nurture their self-esteem. I encouraged Taymor to speak up and let his feelings be known: "While I admire your courage in trying to let the humor run its course, now that you can't deflect the pain, you need to firmly ask them to stop." I advised: "Besides, we all have something we feel vulnerable about; you may just want to remind them of that."

We are not the first American immigrant community to feel vulnerable or to be feared by our neighbors. As American Muslims, my children are but the latest iteration of the American dream, one that has been well traveled by others before them: Catholics, Jews, Japanese, and African Americans, to name a few. I remind my children that the American dream is earned, not given. Americans have been a beacon for the world, and American Muslims now must also be. As Americans and as Muslims we embody that which is quintessentially American in values. We are ethnically diverse: we come originally from seventy-seven different countries—we are Africans, Asians, Croatians, Turks, Kurds, Chinese, and Arabs, to name a few ethnicities—and we don't all look the same. We are quintessentially American in the way that, as a minority, we depend on constitutional rights and inalienable truths for protection and dignity. As eager new patriots, we energize and invigorate the American dream by holding the country we love accountable to its highest ideals of justice and equality for all.

These ideals are challenged sometimes by genuine fear and other times by political and personal agendas that harness people's fears for gain. Scrutiny is one thing, but inflammatory vitriol is another. It makes me worry that my children's sense of belonging to America as Americans could be compromised. My worry is not just out of a concern for their emotional happiness and well-being, but also for the dangers that alienation can breed in sensitive, vulnerable young adults. As a family we do not look particularly ethnic, and we don't wear any outward symbols of our religion. Yet my children have been labeled and judged. I can only imagine the challenges for those American Muslim children who are more stereotypically Muslim in appearance. When only Al-Qaeda is accepted as the true and authentic Islam and when Islam is branded as a violent religion mandating death and destruction, I fear the pain of that judgment and rejection and the consequences of its ensuing alienation. I wonder if the Islamophobes make it easier for terrorists to find one more vulnerable recruit.

When evangelist Franklin Graham describes Islam as a "very evil and wicked religion," I worry about a whole generation of American Muslim children having to come of age under such suspicion and rejection. When I hear about the Minnesota woman who took the microphone at a national religious Right prayer rally in Washington, DC, to pray, "And, Father, we repent that we have not used godly wisdom when we have elected officials into elected positions in our state and nation, Father, and that it has opened the door; that Minnesota holds the responsibility for placing the first Muslim in Congress, and, for that, God, we repent," I second-guess my optimistic faith in a better future for my children. When the interviewer Glenn Beck asks Keith Ellison, the first American Muslim to be elected to Congress, to prove to him that he was "not working for the enemy," I worry about how these questions will affect young, impressionable, and vulnerable American Muslims. I try to teach my children to be empathetic when it comes to people's fears. "If you did not know any Muslims and you only knew about Islam through the headline news, you might feel that way," I say. "It is human to fear that which we don't know or understand." Still, it stings when I'm reminded that even the direction Muslims face when they pray—toward Mecca—is feared. Because of it, some question their loyalty as American citizens. But I also warn them about those who try to use those fears for political gain. Although it was difficult to watch, we sat down in front of the TV together and saw parts of Peter King's congressional hearings, which reduced Congressman Keith Ellison to tears as he testified in defense of his faith and community. The tension between my children's identities as Americans and as Muslims was raw and throbbing with confusing emotions. The idealism of their youth and its open-ended hope was censored by realities out of their control. Are they as American as other Americans?

Every time there is a Jihad Jane or a Fort Hood massacre—or a would-be underwear bomber or a potential car bomb in the

middle of Times Square—these assumptions and fears are fortified. "Just what we need," my son sighs in exasperation as he
catches a news clip of five radicalized Muslim men from northern
Virginia who had traveled to Pakistan in search of jihad, "another
example of Muslims doing something bad." My travels on behalf
of *The Faith Club* have taught me that for many, the fear of Muslims is real. My ultimate goal is to empower my children. I do
not want them to feel like victims. A part of their identity will be
defined in opposition to pervasive stereotypes, and they will face
issues that other Americans may not face. Ideally, they will rise
to the challenge and embrace their identity's inherent tensions as
they try to personify a better tomorrow. Armed with truth, they
can be proud Americans who honor their country and their faith
without for a second believing that there is an inherent contradiction between the two. I worry about the alternative being a sense
of shame or a denial of heritage and lowered self-esteem. When I
have expressed these concerns to Jewish friends, they immediately
understand and relate to my fears. Generations of Jewish children
grew up feeling that they had to apologize for being Jewish as they
defined their identities in opposition to anti-Semitic stereotypes
or, from fear of pogroms, concealed their Judaism.

I am careful not to demand that my children persevere as
Muslims. Ultimately, the choice of faith and identity must be
theirs. They will need to find out for themselves what, at the end
of the day, it means for them to be American and Muslim. I can
only help clarify, give them some of the answers they are looking

for along the way. My hope is that they feel a sense of purpose and pride in their final choice. This year, Leia had to fill out the form for her SAT II biology subject test. The paperwork was online. I watched with pride as she checked the box identifying herself as Muslim. Taymor, who is younger and more sensitive by nature, was for a while not as certain. The teasing and the taunts were still alive and well at school. As part of their history curriculum the boys were studying the Middle Ages. To enrich their experience of the unit, they watched films and documentaries about that historical time period. Taymor was upset because he did not understand why every time there was Muslim character or prayer, some of the boys would poke fun at the beards or garb or rituals. "They don't make fun of the Jews that way, Mom, and they wouldn't make fun of someone's skin color," he remarked. "Don't they know how it makes me feel?" he complained. "I wouldn't do it to them."

Every year Taymor's school puts on a Medieval Feast with elaborate costumes, music, and food as part of the history unit. The boys are very excited when they are knighted. As part of the knighting ceremony, for homework, the boys are asked to write a pledge. Ten words are to be constructed in sentences that convey qualities that a knight may possess. My heart skipped a beat as I read my son's first self-proclaimed knightly quality about an incident he had never before shared with my husband or me. "I showed courage," he wrote, "when an older boy asked me, when he found out that I was a Muslim, if I celebrated 9/11—and I did not get angry."

This program also included a re-enactment of a fight between the Muslim Saladin and Richard the Lionheart performed by two appropriately costume-clad teachers. In the past, Saladin was booed, but this year the boys were asked to honor both as "worthy foes." I wondered if the school had recognized that what had in the past seemed like an innocent and fun reenactment of a historical battle between the "good Christian" and the "bad Muslim" could have inadvertently challenged Taymor's American Muslim identity. Grateful for the modification, I never asked. The boys were also asked to create their own knightly banners, which were used to decorate the walls of the assembly room as it was transformed into a medieval great hall for the big day. I watched my son struggle with how to personalize and decorate his banner. Some boys had family crests; others were quick to use a Star of David or a cross as the centerpiece. Taymor felt less certain and was slow to commit. I was careful not to influence his choice. On the day of the feast, I couldn't help but smile and think of my Omaha friend as my very American son eagerly asked, "Mom, have you seen my banner?" "Yes, it looks great," I replied, as I surveyed the colorful American renditions, hanging side by side in the assembly room, of crosses, Stars of David, and my son's crescent and star.

As Taymor matures, he continues to gain confidence in the nuances and complexities of his identity. Symbols and drawings have become words as he continues to find his voice. His latest English assignment was an opportunity for him to share with his classmates his true feelings about the years of teasing he had tried to pass off as funny or benign. The English teacher had asked them to write a rhyming poem about a single theme. As I ran out the door on a Saturday, I suggested that he might want to write about a theme that is important to him or that he feels passionately about. When I read it, I knew that no matter the challenges that lie ahead, Taymor was well on his way to carrying his identity with dignity and pride. As a parent, that is all I can hope for. This is what he read aloud to his class:

Building Character

I stare into the mirror
Dressed up in my school's blue.
No, I do not bring terror;
I am just like all of you.
American, born and raised,
It's from where I originate.
My box of dates are not grenades,
And 9/11, I do not celebrate.
"Osama's grandson"; I've heard them all.
"Stop, I tell them"; my attempt fails.
It makes it hard to stand tall.
"Shake it off," they say; to no avail.
Stereotypes are many,
Sometimes funny; still they pierce.
Jews and money, Asians are nerdy,

★ **IN GOD WE TRUST** ★

They can be hurtful and fierce.
So let us end this kerfuffle;
Please try not to alienate,
So that no one is in a ruffle,
Stereotypes must abate.

SEVEN

How to Beat a Wife

Verily, God does not change a situation of people until they change what is in themselves.

—Quran 13:11

SOMETIMES, NONE OTHER THAN FELLOW MUS-
lims crush my children's burgeoning voices as proud American Muslims in the most challenging and most spiritually corrosive ways. I am left sinking, backpedaling, searching for answers: not just to their questions, but also to my own. Too often, it is other Muslims who are the source of our angst. Muslims wedded to an imagined orthodoxy, developed in seventh-century Arabia, make it easier for those who are intent on vilifying and damning all Muslims. They provide rich material, ripe for the picking, for those who are far too eager to condemn Islam as an obsolete religion, those who fail to appreciate that Islam is not Communism—a

man-made ideology that can be bled dry—but a religion revered as God's word by over 1.6 billion people. As a result, Muslims who embrace the faith first and foremost because of their belief in its justice and dignity remain unheard, at least by the average American. My last book club meeting left me grappling with this issue.

It had been a long day, and I was looking forward to the aromatic poached salmon and red pepper soup garnished with chunky croutons that our hostess had just served. My appetite, however, was about to be arrested by a friendly warning delivered by a well-meaning mom. Her son, a year ahead of mine at school, had a quiz on the Islam unit in his history book. "I thought of you the other day; next year Taymor will be learning about Islam in history class. The book teaches that Islam sanctions wife beatings."

I thanked her for her concern and casually scooped a spoonful of red pepper soup, hoping that I would not choke or betray my mounting panic as I pictured Taymor in class next year with all eyes turning to him as the teacher explained how Muslims were allowed to beat their wives. I made a mental note: "Check out fifth-grade history book." Surely there is an easy answer to this allegation. There could not possibly be any moral ambiguity on the issue of wife beating. Not in this day and age, I reassured myself. After all, Islam had not invented misogyny. Other faith traditions have had to address scriptures and religious laws that have been less than generous to women, I reasoned. Surely, a little time surfing the Internet for perspective and information would help me put the issue to rest before a reasonable bedtime. Late into the night, I continued staring at my computer screen, gripped by my worst fears, enraged by the vile reasoning and the injustice and cruelty that were masquerading as Islam.

I watched an animated cleric revel in the delivery of his sermon, fervently parsing one of the Quran's most controversial verses: "We must know that wife beating is a punishment in Islamic law. No one should deny this because it was permitted by the Creator of Man," he defiantly warned. Now that he was warmed up, he continued:

We shouldn't be ashamed before the nations of the world to admit that these beatings are part of our law. . . . The Quran says: 'And beat them'—this is a wondrous verse. There are three types of women with whom life is impossible without beatings; unless he carries a rod on his shoulder. The first type is a woman who was brought up that way . . . so she became accustomed to beatings . . . we pray Allah will help her husband later. The second type is a woman who is condescending towards her husband and ignores him. With her, too, only a rod will help. The third type is a twisted woman who will not obey her husband, unless he oppresses her, beats her, uses force against her.[1]

As hard as I prayed, I knew I had not stumbled on a lone preacher being aired on some radical network. He was not the only Muslim on the Internet preaching this position. I quickly learned that the troublesome verse has Muslims divided into three different categories of approach in interpretation. This first approach, embraced by the literalists and Wahhabis, is the one that had kept me up horrified late into the night.

The second approach, embraced by apologists, tries to whitewash the verse by offering conditions and qualifiers regulating and limiting the circumstances under which a Muslim husband can beat his wife. Muslims who use this approach prefer to use euphemisms such as "tap" or "beat lightly." They emphasize that the measure is an extreme, to be used only as an absolute last resort when all other efforts and necessary other steps have failed to hold sway. A husband, we are told, must first try to admonish his wife, then he may try leaving the conjugal bed, and only when these preliminary steps have failed can he resort to "tapping" her lightly. Again as a way of whitewashing the verse, conditions are placed on how and to what degree. A wife should not be hurt, the husband cannot break bones or cause his wife to bleed or to bruise, and he must avoid her face and other sensitive parts of her body. The "tap" should be equivalent to being hit by a toothpick or toothbrush. I find this approach tragic and comically absurd in its desperate efforts to resolve a Quranic verse that is clearly offensive—even to those defending it. Its proponents understand that the verse is unacceptable to the social and cultural values of the twenty-first century, but they are not ready to make that leap which requires the rejection of a verse that is in the Quran.

Progressive and reform-minded Muslims embrace the third approach. These are Muslims who understand that, first and foremost, the Quran needs to be read as a whole in the context of the time and culture of its revelation. When there are seemingly contradictory or ambiguous verses, they read them in deference to the most important value expounded in the Quran: justice. They take heart in the fact that the Quran has an overwhelming number of verses calling on its faithful to use their heads and minds, reminding us that the Quran itself asserts that "there are some verses that are absolute and unequivocal, and others that are alligorical and equivocal."[2] The wife-beating verse clearly belongs to the latter. A few years ago, Dr. Laleh Bakhtiar made headline news as the first American woman to translate the Quran. She took issue with traditional interpretations of the verse in question and removed it from her published translation of the Quran, explaining that for men to beat their wives is a contradiction to the overall message of the absolute justice of God.[3] She also discovered that linguistically the word *darba*, which is the Arabic word for "beat," has seventeen different meanings in the Quran. For the most part it is used to mean "separate" and can even mean to "lay with." Such a translation was made by Ahmed Ali: "As for women you feel are averse, talk to them persuasively; then leave them alone in bed (without molesting them) and go to bed with them (when they are willing)."[4]

As a woman and a mother, the reason I can live another day as a Muslim is that I know that there are passionate and committed

Muslims who are working tirelessly to eliminate any room for
moral ambiguity. There can be none. Those who know better need
to take absolute stands. When the Spanish Imam Mohammad
Kamal Mustafa published a book describing how a husband can
discipline his disobedient wife by using a rod that is thin and light
so that it does not leave scars or bruises on the body, he was given
a fifteen-month sentence for inciting violence against women.
My convictions and commitment to Islam are strengthened—not
weakened—when I am faced with these challenges. They give my
faith purpose and duty: a desire to serve and help those who are
not as fortunate. It is a religious calling of sorts, which, as a mother,
I hope my children in their own ways can fulfill. Our mission is to
help foster and reclaim the ideals of our faith; our cause is a spiritual gift. Our lives are enriched and fulfilled when, through our
voices or actions, we engage—not escape. The solution is not the
desertion of Islam but rather an immersion in Islam as we strive
to reconnect with the "righteous path." I shudder at the thought
that there may be Muslim women out there being battered and
silently accepting physical punishment because they are told that
it is in the Quran—an article of faith. Its moral depravity is akin
to arguing that since slaves are mentioned in all three scriptures,
slavery is sanctioned. Taking a lighter approach are progressives
such as the Turkish Fethullah Gülen, who has a global network
of millions of followers. His response, although tongue in cheek,
delivers the message: women should take up karate, tae kwon do,
or judo, so that "if he hits once, she should hit him twice."[5]

Wife battering knows no religion. In America, 22 percent of marriages cite domestic violence as the cause of divorce. The surgeon general's office has shown domestic violence to be the leading cause of injury to women between the ages of fifteen and forty-four: more common than automobile accidents, muggings, and cancer deaths combined. Every year, domestic violence results in almost 100,000 days of hospitalizations.[6] No just God would sanction the use of violence as a basis for marriage. Muslims know that their God does not either.

EIGHT

Who Speaks for Islam?

Indeed there is no excellence for an Arab over a non-Arab or a non-Arab over an Arab, or a white person over a black one, or a black person over a white one, except through piety.

—The Prophet Muhammad

THE WIFE-BEATING ADVOCATES I HAD DIS-covered online believe that they are speaking for Islam, which naturally begs the question: Who really does speak for Islam? The wife-beating advocates or Muslims like us? The Saudis, many of whom have conflated their tribal morals into their understanding of Islam, or Muslims from over fifty majority states including Turkey, Indonesia, and Malaysia, as well as Muslim minorities in China, Russia, and France? Are Saudis, or any other Muslims, for that matter, more Muslim than others? I was at the Union Theological Seminary when my unveiled Muslim head and I were challenged by this very question. Suzanne, my Faith Club co-author, was pursuing a graduate degree in theology at the seminary when she invited me to co-present to her class. "I have a feeling that the class may only get to hear from one perspective, and I would like you to be there as an expression of the diversity of Muslims in America," she explained. I jumped at the opportunity to take a break from my routine and to spend some time in an academic setting, an environment that I have always found invigorating. It was an intimate class, and my fellow (veiled) Muslim and I sat next to each other, facing our small audience. After brief introductions, she began describing her view of "the Muslim life": Muslim women must cover their heads as a sign of modesty and chastity to ensure that they don't sexually entice men other than their husbands; Muslim women do not shake hands with men. I began to squirm physically. I felt belittled in my faith, unrecognizably and illegitimately Muslim according to her dictums, even as I sat next to her as a representative of the faith. I could no longer contain myself. No amount of lip biting or counting to ten could restrain what I was about to blurt out. "Excuse me," I interrupted her in mid-sentence, "do you mind if you stop saying Muslim women and instead say orthodox Muslim women? Because when you say Muslim women it makes me feel like I am not a Muslim." "As long as you call yourself a progressive Muslim" was her conditional answer. I'll take that.

The tension between orthodoxy and spirituality, between those who place the highest religious premium on obedience to rules and rituals and those who find their religious calling in more spiritual and cultural quests, is not exclusive to Islam. There is a bias that tends to presume that religiosity and a strict observance of rituals are more authentic markers of faith and belief. Still, for the most part, the diversity and plurality in approach to worship is accepted and recognized for different types of Christians and Jews. Generally, if you are Jewish or Christian, you are not told that you do not look Christian or Jewish based on your clothing. For Muslims, and especially American Muslims, this is not the case. It is no wonder then that my children and I continue to be asked if we are really Muslims or told that we do not look Muslim—a remark that, even when made in good faith, hints at the hurdles and issues that plague my children's identities. This is because the majority of Americans continue to paint Islam with one brushstroke, unaware that diversity within Islam is as much a reality as it is within Jewish and Christian communities. My children's Islam and their self-identification as Muslims are vulnerable not only to outsiders' stereotyping, but even more importantly to other Muslims who have designated themselves the gatekeepers of Islam and who are eager to dismiss my children as Muslims.

The reasons are many. Reasons that fortify my convictions about the importance of Muslims like us not accepting the idea that they can be denied the right to identify as Muslims. Islam's most recent chapter in history has been one that is sustained and nurtured by billions of petrodollars in an effort to establish one monolithic absolute path defined by Wahhabi orthodoxy. Its ultimate goal has been to Saudify Islam. Segregation and the ban on women driving or traveling without their husbands' permission are better understood as tribal traditions infused with misogyny. Saudi tribal and cultural orthodoxy has been peddled as Muslim orthodoxy to the point where even Muslims have a hard time recognizing what is Muslim and what is not. I have actually heard Muslims wonder whether Sufis are Muslims. Saudi Arabia's historical and geographical connections to Islam are worn as authenticity badges and credentials of Muslim superiority in efforts to Saudify other Muslims and impose conformity to a national Saudi Muslim brand. But Islam is not a nationality. It never was one national identity. It continues to flourish and be nourished by the diversity of nationalities and cultures from east to west and north to south. Islam is so much bigger than a specific set of cultural markers or a specific headdress. It is so much more than that.

There are Muslims who are continuously in search of an absolute and monolithic orthodoxy, who sacrifice critical thinking. They are preoccupied with punitive laws, with what is *haram,* or not Islamically sanctioned. Their preoccupation with the "Muslim form" has replaced substance; the trivial has replaced the fundamental and the quest for justice. In their hands, Islam is punitive, reduced to what you *cannot* do as opposed to what you can do. Islam becomes a prohibitive and limiting path to life instead of an unrestrictive, open faith inspiring and empowering Muslim women and men to serve, heal, solve, and innovate. The former is not the Islam I choose for my children; it is a choice I am privileged to make because we are American. There are Muslims who have replaced the worship of God with the worship of religion as defined by them, which is in its extreme a form of self-worship. As arbitrators of the faith, they give themselves the power to standardize and control its cultural expression. My children are American Muslims, just as there are Indonesian, Turkish, Chinese, and European Muslims. To reduce Islam to all that is non-Western is not only a fallacy but by definition breeds reactionary positions. The ultimate quest then becomes the search for an elusive orthodoxy, defined 1,400 years ago in the deserts of Arabia, as opposed to a forward-thinking ethic of a global religion. Muslims need a confident ethic, propelled by the pursuit of social justice, which can ultimately help them navigate the plurality and diversity of their experiences as global citizens of the twenty-first century.

If the Saudis don't speak for Muslims, then who does? No one does. Islam is universal in its founding ethos and not confined by territorial premises or ethnic markers. To allow Saudis to claim Islam on the basis of its early nascent history is akin to claiming that Christianity is to be defined only by its embryonic geographical history in Palestine. When Americans who are uncomfortable with Islam ask Muslims to go "back to Mecca," they presume that Muslims belong to a Muslim Saudi homeland, which is a complete fallacy. Islam is a universal religion that is as colored and varied as the hundreds of communities and cultures in which it thrives. Each tells a story and a narrative that is related to the experiences and needs of its followers: from African American Muslims to Turkish mystics and Sufis.

Sunni Muslims, who represent 90 percent of Muslims, have no official clergy who act as intermediaries between the individual and God. Islam does not have one Muslim head or a single religious authority that represents all Muslims. So when Americans complain about Muslims not speaking up, part of the problem is that there is no official Muslim spokesperson or one official Muslim organization that can uphold unequivocal positions for all Muslims.

When Taymor was in grade school, he worried that, although he is American by birth, his foreign-sounding name would deny him the opportunity to be flag-bearer, an honor that boys look forward to at his school on assembly days. His feelings of "otherness" are accentuated by many in America who have expressed concern over the loyalty of American Muslims to the Constitution and American values. This is a fear that is misplaced in its assumptions that there is a monolithic cultural expression of Islam with values that run counter to American values of freedom and diversity and that are sustained by some overarching religious head or organization that competes for Muslim loyalty. Put simply, Muslims have neither pope nor Vatican. American Muslim loyalties are to God and country. To a God who is universal, egalitarian, neither black nor white, neither Eastern nor Western, neither male nor female; and to a country united as one nation, under God, indivisible, with liberty and justice for all.

I am fiercely independent in spirit. The appeal of a direct relationship with God, unencumbered by a religious hierarchy, is vital to my faith as a Muslim. I recently came across an interview with Lady Evelyn Cobbold, a British convert to Islam who in 1933 became the first British woman to perform the pilgrimage to Mecca. When she was asked why she became a Muslim, she described Islam as "a religion of common sense" that fortified her innate belief that Moses, Jesus, and Muhammad were all prophets divinely inspired and that to every nation God sent an apostle. She believed that "we do not need any redemption, that we do not need anyone to intercede between us and God, Whom we can approach at all times, and that no one can intercede for us, not even the Holy Prophet Muhammad, or Jesus, and our salvation depends on ourselves and on our actions."[1] Her convictions speak for my faith. Today, Islam and Muslims could not be any further from that truth. Islam's authority vacuum has allowed everyone and anyone to co-opt God to their cause and invoke the name of God. From the state that has used the pulpit and religious authority to legitimize its power to the rebels and radicals who want to dismantle the state's power and the vilest of terrorists. As a result, the question of who speaks for Islam is open-ended and confusing for Muslims and non-Muslims alike. In theory, the absence of religious intermediaries in Islam was intended to foster a closer relationship between the individual and God, and to eliminate the dangers of individuals monopolizing God and acting as God's gatekeepers. In practice, this is not working. Today there is a proliferation of self-appointed ambassadors to God, demigods, and demagogues, whose only credentials are often that they have grown a beard and wear a turban. These bearded and turbaned experts are preaching to an audience that has failed in its personal religious duty to read "in the name of God." The level of religious literacy among many Muslims is dumbfounding. After all, the first word of the Quran is "Read." Muslims, perhaps more than any other faith, are called upon to rise to the spiritual challenge of reading and thinking for themselves. The dire Muslim condition is perhaps best summed up with how even the word "read" is now translated into "recite." Blind, unthinking recitations are given, often by young Muslims who commit the Quran to memory for the honor of being known as *hafiz* (a term used to describe those who have memorized the Quran completely) in a language—Arabic—that they don't understand. It is not without reason, then, that lately I have been wondering if Muslims really do need a pope.

When I was interviewed by Diane Sawyer for a special *20/20* program on Islam, she asked, "Where is your Mandela? Where is your Luther?" "There is no one person who can speak for Islam. There is no Muslim pope," I answered. "So who can impose these reforms?" she asked anxiously. "Is Islam by definition incapable of reform?"[2] In fact, 1.6 billion Muslims can instigate reforms by demanding institutions that are true to the needs and reflect the diversity of Muslims in this century as opposed to an Islam that is trapped in the realities of seventh-century Arabia. My children are part of the solution because in America they can be Americans and Muslims who are empowered and protected when they choose to speak up. They are part of a long American history and tradition of freedom of worship for all. They can be Muslims who do not believe in an Islam that makes the peripheral fundamental and the fundamental trivial and who are empowered by an America that has a deep commitment to the diversity and freedom of worship for all as it has been forged and achieved by many other religious communities before them.

I am passionate about my family's Muslim identity because I refuse to have my children's right to Islam be given to them or taken away from them by others. I take it personally when we are made to feel as if we are lesser Muslims. I want my children to be able to understand that Islam is much bigger and much more than what one group of believers says it must be. One can be an observant Muslim or a progressive or an orthodox Muslim, but one Muslim cannot claim his or her style of worship exclusively over another Muslim, or feel that they can give it or deny it to other Muslims. A Muslim is anyone who chooses to call themselves a Muslim. The rest is up to God, who, I tell my children, is omnipresent. He can see what is in our hearts and minds. I hope to instill in my children a private faith, cultivated and nourished in their hearts, the muscle of life, the chamber of love that pulsates a beat closer to the rhythms of the universe and the secret of the origins of life; and a mind that is nourished by a disciplined quest for the ever-elusive goal of justice for all.

NINE

Foolish Fatwas

Whenever you speak, speak justly, O you who believe stand out firmly for justice, as a witness to God, even as against yourselves, or your parents or your kin, and whether it be against rich or poor.

—Quran 4:135

NOWHERE IS THE CONFUSION OVER WHO speaks for Islam more troublesome than in the proliferation of fatwas (legal decrees in Islam issued by religious law experts) and the fear and confusion they continue to provoke. It was not too long ago that Leia called, appalled: "You won't believe what I just saw." My daughter is now old enough to travel on her own and was making her way to the West Side of Manhattan to meet her friends when she called. "A bus with an ad that says: 'Leaving Islam? Fatwa on your head? Is your family threatening you?' Isn't that so insulting, Mom?" she asked.

Without passing judgment on the motives of Pamela Geller's Stop Islamization of America group, which is behind the ads and insists that it has a sincere desire to protect Muslims, I had my own protecting to do as a mother. I had to help Leia navigate the thorny issues she faces as an American and a Muslim, even when she is just being a teenager out and about town, having fun with friends. I had to help her feel empowered, even as she recognizes that Islam has its fair share of problems: issues within the faith that have made it vulnerable to outside stereotyping and prejudice. "Yes," I replied, "the ads feel insulting to you and to the majority of Muslims, because you know that the majority of Muslims would never dream of using violence and coercion to force a person to stay Muslim. You worry that people might think that is the true nature of your religion, so they judge you, think less of you, or pity you. All those are valid feelings," I confirmed. "But as a committed Muslim, who wants to protect her religion from abuse, it is your job to also understand how some have used fatwas to intimidate and silence. This has made the majority of Muslims vulnerable on all fronts: they are threatened by Muslims who are trying to intimidate and stop them from thinking and speaking freely and by non-Muslims who are convinced that this is the true nature of Islam."

There is no denying that Islam today suffers from a fatwa problem. Fatwas first captured the world's attention and seared my consciousness in 1988 when the author Salman Rushdie was forced into hiding for writing *The Satanic Verses*, a book deemed blasphemous by that epoch's nefarious Muslim: Ayatollah Khomeini. Although it was a potentially fatal fatwa that needed to be taken seriously—since as a man of the cloth and the head of a radical and violent regime, Khomeini commanded the loyalty of hundreds of thousands of ardent followers—I naively hoped it would prove to be a politically motivated anomaly intended to consolidate Khomeini as a revolutionary leader who could defend Islam's honor and stand up to the West. Long before I had children, that fatal fatwa unleashed a deep reserve of emotions and set the stage for many of the identity issues that my children would ultimately face. The conflict was cast in existential terms of irreconcilable values. The West's cherished freedom of speech was threatened by a regressive, intolerant, and violent Islam with a memory of a long history of imperial and colonial conflicts and perceived grievances. The fatwa became a symbol for all that is to be feared about Muslims. For many Muslims, the fatwa became a vengeful tool of liberation, encapsulating centuries of resentment toward Western imperialism and its disregard for Muslim honor and dignity. An author's writing a book was no longer an individual act of freedom of expression, but rather the tipping point for large-scale Muslim resentment at being aggrieved and dishonored at the hands of the West.

It has been twenty-five years since that ominous fatwa set its fatal example, and the preponderance today of foolish fatwas is a source of frustration and shame for the majority of Muslims. So much so that when I share with friends that I will be writing about foolish fatwas, they half-jokingly suggest that I should publish under a pseudonym. They have good reason to worry, since without an official process that can regulate who can issue a fatwa or when a fatwa is legitimate, anyone and everyone can issue a fatwa. The Danish cartoons, the *South Park* episode that had Muhammad in a bear suit and was censored as a result, and the Seattle cartoonist who suggested an "Everyone Draw Muhammad Day" to protest censorship and support the *South Park* cartoonists have all elicited violent threats and reactions. Recently, Pakistan blocked Twitter because of its refusal to block access to tweets that supported "Draw Muhammad Day." These reactions seek to impose, with blood and violence, respect for the Prophet and Islam. They have done nothing but bring shame and dishonor to Islam. Maybe we are not so much created in the image of God as much as we create a God who is in our image. Politically violent and repressive civil societies produce a culture of violence and intolerance. Insecure, intolerant, violent individuals will believe in a God who is insecure, intolerant, and violent. In their hands, Islam is hateful, vicious, and fanatical. As the Algerian writer Ahlam Mosteghanemi lamented, "A man spends his first year learning how to speak and the Arab regimes teach him silence for the rest of his life."[1] The winds of change are sweeping through many Muslim countries in the form of popular revolutions dubbed the Arab Spring. My hope is that these changes will develop civil societies where the sanctity of human life and the diversity of opinion are protected and guaranteed as universal, human, and

Muslim rights. These changes are not proving easy to guarantee or secure in the form of functioning democratic governments and the rule of law and order. No matter how long and arduous the process may prove to be, the Arab Spring has confirmed that these societies are desperate for governments that will treat their people as protected citizens and not arbitrarily as subjects.

Nowhere is the need for responsible citizenship more flagrant than in what has become a comedy of routinely issued bizarre and foolish fatwas. Some fatwas have sanctioned women breastfeeding their adult male co-workers in order to freely intermingle and work in their company, with the idea that doing so will establish a maternal bond between the women and their male colleagues. Others threaten with death the owners of a television station for airing programs deemed inappropriate. Without a system of checks and balances, or a centralized global board or council that can review fatwas before they are issued, fatwas have become a trigger-happy process, a big business. Islam has suffered as a consequence of complete and radical free-market fatwa deregulation. Anyone interested can wake up in the morning and decide to issue a fatwa. Some have been absurd, others have been threatening and dangerous, and all have made the majority of Muslims feel vulnerable and sometimes just plain embarrassed. The proliferation of the Internet and global media has added to the problem. There are e-fatwas being dispensed over the Internet and television programs that have a dial-a-fatwa feature. Some fatwas completely contradict each other, and consumers can literally shop for fatwas that suit their needs. Fatwas are issued on sexual matters and aired on prime-time television in Muslim countries. The topics covered are so intimate and graphic that I am left blushing, wondering at the audacity of it all, in such presumably conservative and traditional societies. Do Muslims really need a fatwa on everything from brushing their teeth to how they socialize? Or when and how to have sex with their spouses? What some of these people need are parents, not Muslim legal opinions. By engaging in the trivial and the banal, Islam becomes a trivial and banal religion. By issuing death threats under the guise of Islamic opinion, Islam becomes a violent religion.

There are Muslims who, in defense of Islam, try to trivialize fatwas. They may even see them as a form of free speech—a point of view I was introduced to when a friend took issue with a Twitter link I had posted to what I believed was a preposterous and embarrassing fatwa. This friend, whom I had not seen since high school, protested: "They are just opinions, edicts, with no legal recourse. No one listens to them." He continued, "'Real' Muslims dismiss them and the outside world uses them to discredit Islam. Are you not for their equal right to express themselves? I think the West is just looking for any issues to disdain." Let's be clear: opinions that threaten, blackmail, and encourage violence qualify as hate speech and should have nothing to do with God and religion. To argue that these fatwas, no matter how outrageous or silly, have no consequences is disingenuous and simply not true. Utterances and words do have consequences. Words have power.

They define our consciousness, enable our thoughts, and express our identities. Foolish fatwas lower the bar of our cultural consciousness and make us vulnerable. We are forced to react, defend, and explain what should be common sense and unequivocal. Words can make the licit illicit, the natural unnatural, and they can be used to create paranoia and taboos, especially when these words are uttered by those who represent themselves as experts on or officials of Islam.

Muslims should not be complacent about what fringe personalities say or issue in the name of Islam. Concern over fatwas is gaining momentum. Hillal Hissa, a Saudi poet, caused a stir when she read a poem that lashed out against violent fatwas in a poetry competition aired on national TV:

I have seen evil from the eyes of the subversive fatwas . . . a monster appears from his hiding place; barbaric in thinking and action, angry and blind; . . .

He speaks from an official, powerful platform, terrorizing people and preying on everyone seeking peace; the voice of courage ran away . . . [2]

Let this generation's courageous voices be heard so that Muslims no longer have to live at the mercy of the next foolish fatwa.

TEN

"Mommy, Sometimes I Don't Want to Support the US Team"

And God loves the ones who are doers of good.

—Quran 3:148

2012 WAS A BIG SUMMER FOR SPORTS FANS like my son. The Olympics were around the corner and so was the European soccer league championship. My son, an avid athlete and a keen sports spectator, asked me a question that succinctly encapsulates his evolving identity struggles and his identity's inherent tensions. A teenager now, he has taken to doodling a crescent and star on his exam papers for good luck, and I have even seen a few *Bismillahs* or "In the name of God"s scribbled beneath. Recently, as we were being dropped off at home after a lacrosse game, I saw a crescent and a star colored in black ink on the inside of his wrist. I was not sure what to make of this ardent display of religious identity, but when he asked me, "Mommy, do I always have to support the US teams?" I became positively worried. "Why wouldn't you?" I asked anxiously, realizing for the first time how sensitive my assimilation radar was. "Because there are very few Muslim athletes who do well, and when they do, I would like to be able to root for them." I was relieved to hear that this was a case of benign Muslim empathy for a religious identity that he perceives as underrepresented and underprivileged in sports rather than a case of alienation or a more callous disregard for national identity. A little like Jewish pride and support for a Jewish athlete at a time when Jewish athletes were few and far between, I thought.

Still, his question unintentionally exposed deeper-rooted tensions that sit uncomfortably at the precipice of the duality of his identity. Many American Jews profess a loyalty or at the very least goodwill toward the welfare of the state of Israel. Israel's former ambassador to the United States, Michael B. Oren, is an American citizen who gave up his American citizenship when he became Israel's ambassador. The synergy between the two countries is such that most Americans would not dream of holding that against him or accusing him of treachery or disloyalty, which might not be the case if he were a Muslim. Americans do not perceive a threat or question American Jewish loyalties because the majority of Americans share the same feelings; there is no tension rooted in either long-held historical perceptions or more expedient political realities. Israel is America's kindred spirit in the Middle East, a relationship nourished by religious, cultural, and political connections.

For American Muslims, it is much more complicated. Since Islam is not confined to one geographical state or country, we become vulnerable to what is said in the name of Islam, anywhere and everywhere. Since there are fifty-seven Muslim majority states and significant minorities globally, American Muslims can find themselves beholden to the actions and beliefs of other Muslims anywhere from Afghanistan to the Philippines. American Muslims may not identify or recognize their faith as practiced in the hands of other Muslims, but they are nevertheless held accountable for the actions and utterances of other Muslims. I cringed as I listened to Eboo Patel, an American Muslim author and interfaith social worker, taking questions from callers for an NPR interview. One caller in particular took issue with Eboo for exalting the value of his identity as both an American and a Muslim. "Why don't you speak about your Islam in Saudi Arabia or Kenya and see how they receive you there?" The caller continued his barrage with, "You should leave America alone." The poignancy of the moment and its tragic irony were highlighted in Eboo's response: "I am an American, and this is my home," delivered in a flawless American accent, in contrast to the caller's heavily accented immigrant English.

America is my family's home too, and we have no other home. There is no overarching Muslim state that promises a right of return to its "promised Muslim lands." Islam is not a nationality, but a faith, as diverse and varied as its 1.6 billion adherents. It is misleading to draw conclusions about American Muslims based on how other Muslims around the world behave. Sadly, though, in America today, there is an entire industry financed and supported by think tanks, authors, filmmakers, and individual vigilantes whose sole purpose is to vilify and spread fear about all things Muslim. If we are to hold Muslims accountable for the possible consequences of their foolish utterances or violent threats—as we rightly should—we must do the same to others who are also in the business of inciting fear through gross inflammatory language and hateful stereotypes. I am an absolute and unequivocal believer in an individual's right to freedom of speech. Many American Muslims who are recent immigrants have experienced firsthand life in societies where fear, intimidation, and violence are used to muzzle a person's right to his or her free and expressed opinion. As such, they intimately relate to Evelyn Beatrice Hall's "I disapprove of what you say, but I will defend to the death your right to say it." We also understand that this sacred American right is a revered gift that was not guaranteed overnight but earned, developed, and protected through judicial, political, and legal systems that matured and evolved over time, institutions and systems that are sorely lacking in much of the Muslim world. However, even advocates of the absolute necessity of free speech can question and criticize the judgment and the intentions of those who engage in such inflammatory stereotypes. In our home, these jabs deliver bruising punches; they are a blood sport, made more painful because it is played by those whom we want so badly to accept and respect us as fellow Americans: politicians, journalists, and sometimes our next-door neighbors.

My family and I cannot help but take these blogs, movies, and actions personally. To borrow from my son's lingo, it feels like a case of the US team not supporting us. What started out as extreme fringe groups in the aftermath of 9/11—bloggers and writers on the Far Right playing on America's fears and insecurities—has gone mainstream and, most recently, viral. On buses, in subway stations, or, more ominously, on widely viewed YouTube clips, there are efforts to denigrate, insult, and offend. Whereas before we could choose to ignore these offenses or switch them off at the click of a button to protect our children from their gross allegations and misconceptions, today they are an inescapable part of the national conversation. Michele Bachmann, Republican member of the House of Representatives and briefly a candidate for the Republican Party's presidential nomination, wrote a letter to the US State Department suggesting that it is compromised by the influence of the Muslim Brotherhood, whose mission is to destroy Western civilization from within—a form of civilization jihad. In what read like a McCarthy-worthy witch hunt, she accused Huma Abedin, Hillary Clinton's intelligent and accomplished Muslim aide, of having possible ties to the Muslim Brotherhood. If that narrative is not worthy of a James Bond thriller, then the visuals in the film *The Third Jihad: Radical Islam's Vision for America*—played on a continuous loop over three months as officers were recruited for the NYPD, as uncovered in January 2011[1]—just might be. This film features bloody footage of executed children and an Islamic flag flying over the White House while the narrator explains that "this is the true agenda of much of Islam in America." This widespread anti-Muslim propaganda is financed with millions of dollars by dubious nonprofit organizations (such as Clarion), associated with the gambling magnate Sheldon Adelson, who has definitive political biases and positions on American foreign policy, especially as it pertains to Israel and the Middle East.

Whereas in my youth I would have been insulted or angered by some of these preposterous positions and remarks, today, as a mother, I am more than anything deeply saddened and concerned for my children and the tough road that lies ahead. The emotional havoc these attacks may wield on American Muslim families pales in significance when the devastating implications of such inflammatory positions are considered in their global context. They become the fuel and fodder that feed the imagination of the less than stable and the violent—a violence not confined to Muslims. Norway's Anders Behring Breivik, who gunned down seventy-seven victims, many of whom were children, remained defiant and true to his motives through his trial, believing his actions necessary and crucial to prevent the "creeping Muslim takeover of Europe." Many of his ideas, political fears, and anxieties were aided and abetted by American Islamophobic bloggers Pamela Geller and Robert Spencer, whom he mentioned by name in the 1,500-page manifesto that he posted online. On the home front, we have not been immune to violence from white supremacists or, in a case of possible mistaken religious identities, the gunning down of six people at a Sikh temple in Wisconsin. Other incidents have been minor in comparison, limited to cases of vandalism and arson, such as in Missouri, where a mosque was burned down.

Sadly, hate speech is an equal-opportunity instrument; whether it is anti-American or anti-Christian or anti-Jewish or anti-Muslim, it can play equally into the fears, anxieties, and indignities of those who are inclined to be violent or are less than emotionally stable, triggering often deadly conclusions. I have heard friends express bewilderment as to how an amateurish, lampoon-ish, badly produced trailer depicting the Prophet Muhammad as a treacherous and lecherous buffoon would not just be seen as trivial; or in the case of offensive cartoons, why they would not be judged as satire in the tradition of *New Yorker* cartoons. These are reasonable assumptions or judgments for Americans, or for those societies that have had centuries of civil rights, the rule of law, and the protection of free speech as fundamental components of their governance. To expect that our American aesthetics of satire and humor and the triviality of the affair should be the order of the day for societies such as Libya's, which have recently gone through revolutions and are still in social and legal turmoil, is not only insular, but quite frankly politically naive. Vigilantes and mob justice, along with religious and political fomenters who make it their business to manufacture and inflame grievances compounded by a history of colonialism and military invasions for personal gain, are the order of the day. In the absence of the absolute rule of law and sound civil institutions such as in Pakistan, the violent protests become predictable. Such indignation and persecution, when suffered by those who are violent, can end in the tragic loss of life. Recently, over dinner, I bemoaned how violent the year 2012 was, with shootings at a movie theater in Aurora, the loss of life at a Sikh temple in Oak Creek, and the school shootings at Newtown, Connecticut; a poignant reminder of how violence knows no boundaries. My host demurely disagreed; he feels that there is a difference in the types of violence. I only hope that what was left unsaid—a nagging suspicion that he may believe that the violence carried out in the defense of Islam is rooted in the nature of Islam as a religion—is not what he truly believes. I see no difference between those who are acting out of fear and hate for Islam and those who act out of fear and hate for America. I make no distinction in death and the loss of life. But I distinguish in the quality of our American civic traditions and societies and our deep commitment to the freedom of all to worship and speak freely, values that the Muslim world needs to respect and that American Muslims rely on for protection at home.

This is protection that is increasingly vital to us since fear and vilification of Muslims have unfortunately not abated, but rather increased, since 9/11. Pamela Geller's organizations, Atlas Shrugs and Stop Islamization of America, have been labeled hate groups by the Southern Poverty Law Center. The film *The Innocence of Muslims*, vehemently promoted by insurance agent and Vietnam War veteran Steven Klein, has sparked violent protests globally, some of which resulted in tragic deaths.[2] We can't help but take their hate personally and be distressed. Geller, whose mandate is to warn Americans about stealth jihad and the invasion of American culture and politics by Muslims, reentered our lives in the fall of 2012 with another ad campaign, this time in New York City subways, soliciting Americans to support the civilized man against the savage by supporting Israel and defeating jihad. Although one can argue that of course we are all against violence, whether it is called jihad or not, subliminally the message is that Israel is civilized and that its enemies, whose land it occupies, are savages. Klein's son is an American soldier who was awarded the Purple Heart for his service in Iraq. I am sure he could at least relate to me as a parent, to understand that I would take issue with having my Muslim children being called pedophiles and wife beaters, as he describes all Muslims in an interview.[3] These activists are so eager to validate those Muslims who are hateful and criminal. Klein and his followers make a habit of taking the most extreme of readings and the most violent and misogynist of Muslims and presenting them as representatives of all Muslims. Exceptions and anomalies are treated as if they are the norm. Exceptional stories of violence in the name of Islam become the true but stealthy, hidden, and sinister face of all Muslims—no matter how many and how much Muslims insist otherwise. This industry and its speakers, authors, and think tanks are determined to rescue Muslims from themselves. They believe that if they keep beating down Muslims by insulting their prophet and their scriptures, Muslims will have an epiphany and realize that they should not be Muslims and thank them for being "saved" from being Muslim. This bizarre logic, the rescue of Muslims from Islam, is the declared intent and goal of the trailer *The Innocence of Muslims,* filmed by a Coptic Christian, Nakoula Basseley Nakoula, who has told the *New York Times* that he would go to great lengths to covey "the actual truth" about Muhammad.

Taymor's question about supporting the US team reminded me of a question he had once asked when he was much younger. As we walked out of the apartment one morning, he caught site of a *New York Times* front-page photo depicting a cowering, blindfolded, and bearded Muslim man being held at gunpoint by an American soldier in Iraq. "Those are the bad guys, right, Mom?" It is not just children who see the world that way: good against evil; either you are with us or against us; superheroes and supervillains; East against West; freedom against oppression; my team or their team. But what if your identity, by virtue of being American *and* Muslim, occupies that space in between? An identity that sits uncomfortably in a reality defined not by good and bad absolutes but rather in nuance and diversity of being: in recognizing that there are good and bad Muslims as there are good and bad Christians. That there is good and bad theology as there are good and bad Muslim Imams and Christian priests. That religions are, at the end of the day, a journey in ethics and humanity, a journey of the daily struggle to achieve proximity to the divine. They are most inspiring when they are lived and practiced ethics fortified in action and by a life of service, not hollowed by arrogance and sanctimonious faith. Those who use their faith to hate and kill and demonize and demand respect are the furthest from the divine. Faith is at its most glorious when it is a journey of love, rendered more meaningful when it is an effort to love those who are most different from us. Growing up is a difficult enough journey; growing up navigating viscous currents outside the convenience of popular absolutes can be treacherous and requires vigilance and effort on the part of parents. It is like growing up in a warring home where the two parents offer conditional love: renounce the other parent so that I can love you fully and completely.

Sometimes, though, the stars align and the answers don't seem so elusive, as when Mohammad (Mo) Farah, a Somali-born British immigrant who trained in America, won successive gold medals in track and field for his adopted country, including Britain's first-ever gold in the 10,000-meter race. He dropped to his knees, prostrating himself in Muslim prayer in front of the world. My son's question about sometimes supporting athletes other than our own became my own. There is so much Western fear of all things Muslim: narratives that reject Muslims and the possibility of Muslim assimilation and integration, and imply the stealthy Muslim encroachment and violation of sacred Western values. I sat there and cried as I watched him thank God. He made me feel so proud to be a Muslim. He provided us with the opportunity to bask in the glow of his success, offered a distinct window of pride and redemption. Had he been an American Muslim, I would never have felt as proud to be an American; I would have been grateful for the rare gift of the celebration of our identities as both proud American and Muslim when so many Americans and Muslims reject me. Watching this British Muslim athlete, I finally truly understood my son's question. He was looking for Muslim athletes who would rescue his beleaguered identity, who would deliver on the promise and hope of all that can be good about Muslims, in a world that more often than not does not celebrate Muslims. When Mohammad Farah dropped to his knees, he became a rare symbol of Muslim pride, and when he wrapped the Union Jack around him, in that moment, he was neither Muslim first, nor British first, but most certainly British, Muslim, and proud.

ELEVEN

Thumbs Up!

It is not righteousness that ye turn your faces towards East or West;
but it is righteousness—to believe in God and the Last Day, and
the Angels, and the Book, and the Messengers; to spend of your
substance, out of love for Him, for your kin, for orphans, for the
needy, for the wayfarer, for those who ask, and for the ransom of
slaves; to be steadfast in prayer, and practice regular charity; to
fulfill the contracts which ye have made; and to be firm and patient,
in pain (or suffering) and adversity, and throughout all periods of
panic. Such are the people of truth, the God-fearing.

—Quran 2:177

WHEN IMAM FEISAL ABDUL RAUF, THE SPIRI-
tual leader of the so-called Ground Zero Mosque, and his wife,
Daisy Khan, asked me to join the board of the American Society
for Muslim Advancement (ASMA), I jumped at the opportunity.

I had first met this dynamic duo almost a decade ago, when we broke a Ramadan fast together at a downtown mosque after the Imam had led evening prayers. At the time, the children were distraught because they had been told by friends at school that the Easter Bunny surely would not pay them a visit. I shared the story, and the Imam laughed, reassuring me that "of course the Easter Bunny should visit Muslim children." I knew right then and there that I had found my Imam. His wife, Daisy, sat next to him, defying all my stereotypes and assumptions about how an Imam's wife should look or act. She was outspoken and articulate, with a neatly coiffed head of black hair, completely uncovered.

A decade on, our friendship had grown. The Imam had officiated at the marriage of two of my cousins, and I had sought his advice and reflections on all matters religious and theological. He was truly an American Imam, pursuing his lifelong mission: the advancement of a progressive and diverse American Islam of the twenty-first century. When I heard about their plan to build a Muslim community center, I rejoiced. Over the years, in my Faith Club discussions, I confessed that I had at times suffered from church and temple envy. I had become familiar with Jewish programs when the children took swimming lessons at the 92nd Street Young Men's and Young Women's Hebrew Association, and I had envied Suzanne's church-sponsored soup kitchen and Sunday school programs. I had even joked with Suzanne and Priscilla that I had sometimes felt like the banished Ishmael when they spoke of the Judeo-Christian tradition.

My hope was that by building Muslim institutions in America, we could help our children to one day be comfortable speaking of the great American Judeo-Christian-Muslim tradition. Although I no longer suffered from feelings of isolation and alienation the way I had right after 9/11, I had yet to find a mosque where I felt comfortable taking my family for religious holidays, but I had found my Imam. Imam Feisal led services on Fridays from a small, modest downtown mosque that was often filled beyond capacity. More often than not, the Imam and Daisy's events were hosted in borrowed spaces, in churches graciously extended for their use or in rented midtown hotel conference rooms. I imagined Imam Feisal's community center as a place that would fill that physical, emotional, and spiritual vacuum and give us a permanent home for conferences and community events. A place where my children could volunteer to serve the neighborhood, feed the hungry, reach out to the community, and build bridges of understanding. A place where my children could celebrate their American values in the context of their Muslim heritage. A place they could point to and say, "Here we are American, Muslim, and proud members of the community." I dreamt of a Muslim Sunday School, a place where they could even shoot hoops and enjoy a swim with a friend or two. A sanctuary, a concrete answer to those who continue to ask, "Where are the moderates?" and a rejection of those who preach a radical and un-American Islam, culturally trapped in seventh-century Arabia. Never did I imagine that the much-hoped-for sanctuary would be the catalyst that would divide the nation and expose America's Islamophobia. For the record, I was not involved in the choice of location for the now-infamous center. Much has been said about the insensitivity and offensiveness of its location. If I thought Islam and not Al-Qaeda was responsible for 9/11, I would feel the same way. I have watched in horror as the gentle Imam—the Imam whom I first met a decade ago at the modest, downtown, Al-Noor mosque, who confirmed that "the Easter Bunny could visit Muslim children"—was accused of being a demagogue, a wolf in sheep's clothing. The controversy has spun out of control and has turned into a "Hate Muslims" fest, with some protestors calling out: "Kill them all!" or "Go back to Mecca!"

There is another point of view, one which must have seemed reasonable for the quiet Imam, who never expected to be at the epicenter of a political storm. When a member of your congregation, who specializes in downtown properties, generously presents a space that seems to be a good economic opportunity, you consider it for many reasons, not the least of which is that you have been in the neighborhood for twenty-five years. You are so engrossed in the world of interfaith relations and bridge building that you are genuine and sincere in the belief that you would like to help rebuild and serve a neighborhood that was devastated by the horror of 9/11. Although close to the site of Ground Zero, the building would not be on it. You may even believe that it would be welcomed as an opportunity to share the true face of Islam in America. The connection between an Imam's religion and spirituality and that of the terrorists is so far removed from reality that it does not occur to you that people might see it as offensive or believe it to be a victory mosque celebrating the terror. Some people have called the Imam naive. Maybe. I prefer to think of him as quintessentially American in his hope, earnestness, and ideals.

The rage and emotions over this issue have run so high that they have put the innocence of my children's childhood at risk. Pundits, blogospheres, and protests have fostered a feeding frenzy of inflammatory positions and hate speech. There have been banners that read, "All I need to know about Islam I learned on 9/11," and prestigious publications such as the *New English Review* have asked "whether Islam is a religion or a political doctrine seeking domination with the veneer of religious practice." The editor in chief of *The New Republic* has declared, "Frankly, Muslim life is cheap, most notably to Muslims. I wonder whether I need to honor these people and pretend that they are worthy of the privileges of the First Amendment, which I have in my gut the sense that they will abuse."[1] Some have insisted that Islam is a cult, not a religion, that it is a threat to our national security and therefore cannot be protected by constitutional rights such as the freedom of worship. It follows, then: cult members or Muslims could lose their constitutional rights. In this climate, even the possibility of internment feels real.

Sometimes, when emotions run so high, the fury is so consuming that we forget that there may be some eleven-year-old boy who has never known a home outside this country, this city, and this neighborhood, but is prematurely thrown into the inferno.

I woke up one recent morning, bleary-eyed, coffee in hand, ready to check my emails. I was in for a rude awakening. The screen screamed at me with YouTube clips and expletive Muslim slurs, the results of a Google search for "I hate Muslims." "Why did you do that?" I reprimanded my son, distressed over what I feared might have been his scarring, non-age-appropriate exposure to hate and foul language. "Oh, I just wanted to see what they say about us," he explained. "I posted a response," he shared, as if to reassure me. This is what he wrote:

> I am a Muslim and I am not a terrorist. Just because one person does something bad, it does not mean it represents a whole religion. Just like Osama Bin Laden does not represent Islam and the people who killed Jesus do not represent Judaism, and like Hitler does not represent Christianity. Just because one person is bad, you can't put him in the name of a religion. And all of you who believe this is true give me a thumbs up.

I worry about which America will receive my children as adults: the America of Sean Hannity and *Fox and Friends,* of jihad watch organizations, and of Tea Party leaders who call Allah the Muslim monkey god? Or the America that serves as a beacon of tolerance and liberty to the world? For now, all I can do is try to protect them from those remarks that I feel are too racist or demoralizing. I am careful to point out that fear and hate are not new to the world. I do not want my children to feel unique or exceptional as victims or targets. Sometimes I explain to them that our need to hate is just as natural and human as our need to love. I point out how we have hated witches, Jews, epileptics, lepers, blacks, and lately, Muslims. Fear readily translates into hate when it is politicized and spun by media demagogues. Hate has a raw, palpable energy that is contagious and is difficult to ignore or rationalize. I came face to face with it when I was asked by Daisy to address the community board before it was to take a vote on the proposed Muslim center. There was a raucous anti-mosque crowd, including a man with a *shofar* (horn), which he blew whenever he felt his side had scored a point. The setting was not for the faint of heart. By the time I was called to address the crowd, my voice was quivering with emotion and fear.

That evening, I was saddened and overwhelmed by the enormity of the challenge that faces my children. During the community board meeting I had been introduced to an Islam that was foreign and completely unrecognizable to me as a Muslim. An Islam that was full of sinister traditions and practices that I had never heard of before. This Islam was presented to me by self-appointed Muslim expert Pamela Geller. Some in the crowd received her like a rock star as she took the microphone and passionately protested the Muslim community center in downtown

New York City. Geller explained why Americans have good reason to fear: "Muslims practice *taqiyah,*" she declared. I looked at
Daisy, perplexed, as the *shofar* blew in approval. "What is that?" I
asked. What is this criminal, sinister practice that I was guilty of
as a Muslim?

I have always wondered whether anti-Semites and racists truly
believe the ridiculous and unimaginable: that Jews drank their
children's blood in matzo ball soup, grew tails, were dirty, untrust-
worthy, weak, and cowardly? Geller seemed sincere enough. Once
we canonize our fear and worship our stereotypes (even those we
make up), the urge to cleanse ourselves, our neighborhoods, and
our country from evil may not be far behind.

I was relieved to go home to the sanctuary of my family, to
leave behind this unrecognizable Islam of *taqiyah, dhimmis,* and
infidels that is a sworn enemy to all Christians and Jews. The
following morning, with the rising sun, I decided to literally put
to the test the advice of the Catholic Al Smith, who said at the
time of his ordeal: "The best way to kill anything un-American is
to drag it out in the open, because anything un-American cannot
live in the sun." I knew I had to drag this Islam of *taqiyahs* and
dhimmis into the sun. Until the fearmongers have a better solution, my family is sticking to clarification—which, by the way,
feels very American.

We decided to look up *taqiyah,* that practice which, according to Pamela Geller, is a Muslim religious duty that calls on
Muslims to deceive and lie to advance their cause. *Taqiyah,* we

soon discovered, refers to an obscure Muslim practice that has historically forgiven Muslims, especially Shias, for denying their Muslim faith if they are faced with the choice of its renunciation or certain death. I am not sure why this is supposed to command fear from fellow Americans, especially since as American Muslims, we do not live in fear of execution for our commitment to our faith. In a manipulation that is Orwellian in proportion and cynicism, *taqiyah* is just one more device used to play on people's genuine fear to harness support for specific political agendas. *Dhimmi* is another word that has been given as evidence of Islam's sinister, criminal ways. A medieval concept, the word refers to the status of Christians and Jews who lived under eighth-century Muslim rule and literally means "the protected." As protected non-Muslims, or *dhimmis,* Jews and Christians were exempt from serving in the army and from paying Muslim alms (*zakat*). Instead, they paid a separate tax to the state. This was all relatively harmless and is frankly irrelevant to Muslims and Islam in America today. In our home, we prefer to celebrate our connections to Jews and Christians. Jesus is one of twenty-five prophets we revere equally in a line of prophets from the Old and New Testaments and a precursor to the Prophet Muhammad. Although Muslims depart from the Christian concept of the Trinity, they believe in Jesus as the messiah, who because of his virgin birth is closest to God in spirit and will sit on his right hand on the Day of Judgment. My favorite verse, which I read frequently to the children, needs no elaboration:

We have sent down the Torah which contains guidance and
light . . . later, we have sent down Jesus, son of Mary, confirming the Torah which was sent down before him, and
gave him the Gospel containing guidance and light. Unto
you (O Muhammad), We have revealed the book (Quran)
with truth. It confirms the scriptures which came before it.[2]

The controversy over the proposed center did not remain geographically confined to its location in New York City. Mosques
and Muslim communities are now being challenged nationally;
some have even been attacked with arson or desecrated (a man
urinated on prayer rugs) in Florida, Tennessee, California, Geor-
gia, Kentucky, Wisconsin, and Illinois, complicating the prospects
and implications of a quiet local relocation. American Muslims
have often worried about the consequences of another terrorist
attack on American soil, but we never anticipated that the slurs
and backlash would be brought home, through the front door of
our neighborhood mosques and centers. Many are gasping for air
as they come to the realization that the implosion is not so much
about bricks and mortar, cement buildings and prayer halls, as
about their very future as individuals and citizens.

The last chapter on the so-called Ground Zero Mosque has
not yet been written. When my children ask if it should be relocated, I tell them that is not the point. It may or it may not
be relocated. What is more important is that America has an
honest dialog. Certain elements of the media have enabled and

perpetrated bigotry against Muslims, and that cannot be good for our country. As Muslims we carry the shame anytime criminals use the name of our religion to perpetrate evil. We understand that we have much work to do from within as we purge extremists and radicals and forge ahead with a progressive, just Islam of the twenty-first century. As Americans we welcome the scrutiny, we are eager to earn your trust, to contribute our sacred values of democracy, freedom, and diversity. To be part of the newest "American faith" chapter in America's long history with civil liberties for its religious minorities. We welcome the dialog, and we trust that America's truth will prevail. It is a truth that manifests itself when you least expect it. An American DNA that is honed by centuries of American values and that is palpable in Imam Feisal's feelings as delivered at a memorial service in memory of the murdered Daniel Pearl:

> If to be a Jew means to say with all one's heart, mind and soul: "Sh'ma Yisrael, Adonai Elohenu Adonei Ehad; Hear O Israel, the Lord our God, the Lord is one," not only today I am a Jew, I have always been one. If to be a Christian is to love the Lord our God with all my heart, mind and soul, and to love for my fellow human being what I love for myself, then not only am I a Christian, but I have always been one.[3]

An American identity that is also confirmed in Mayor Michael Bloomberg's response: "We in New York are Jews and Christians and Muslim, and we always have been. And above all that, we are Americans, each with an equal right to worship and pray where we choose. There is nowhere in the five boroughs that is off-limits to any religion."[4]

I held on to the white (light) one while I gave birth and packed the red (dark) one in my daughter's backpack the morning of September 11, 2001, never imagining that the same Quran I had packed so lovingly would be used to wreak havoc, death, and destruction.

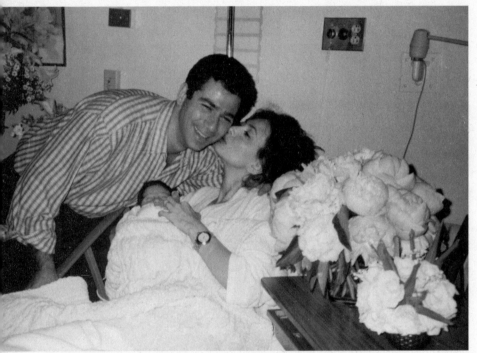

Our daughter, Leia, was delivered by my Jewish doctor (who I had worried would be away for the Jewish holidays) at the New York Hospital in Manhattan, where she was serendipitously paid a visit by New York Hospital's official resident Imam, who whispered the Muslim declaration of faith in her ear, "There is no God but God, and Muhammad is his prophet."

It's okay to be Muslim.

me

It makes me feel weird when I am the only Muslim and everyone around me is either Christian or Jewish.
By Leia Idliby

Leia's first-grade in-class assignment, which caught me off guard when I first saw it. It confirmed that parenting would never be the same. After 9/11, Islam was the elephant in the room; if I chose to ignore it, it would not ignore me.

Leia celebrating the Fourth of July. In spite of my encounter in Omaha, where a gentleman did not feel I qualified as an American, as a family we are passionate about being American, Muslim, and proud.

It is tradition at Taymor's school for a boy to be honored by carrying the American flag during Friday assembly. Taymor worried that his foreign-sounding name would deny him that privilege.

Taymor is an avid athlete who wondered if it was okay to sometimes support a Muslim athlete at the Olympics over an American national. Here he is practicing his all-American baseball swing, although he would ultimately favor basketball and lacrosse.

After The Faith Club, *Christmas traditions I had grown up with were no longer just cultural. I assured Leia and Taymor that, contrary to their friends' claims, Santa does visit Muslim children, for Muslims believe in the virgin birth of Jesus, who is revered as one of twenty-five prophets, and as a Messiah.*

Not only was The Faith Club *embraced in dozens of churches and temples and mosques all across America, but we also made it all the way to Oman, in the Middle East, where we received a warm welcome at the Sultan Qaboos Grand Mosque.*

My parents visiting Jerusalem and the Dome of the Rock for the first time in fifty years since their forced and permanent departure from Palestine in 1948. As a Palestinian refugee, my sixteen-year-old father was bought a one-way ticket to Chicago, where his mission was to get an education.

My father, a toddler, with his parents in happier times. His mother would pass away at the tender age of thirty-eight, medically from kidney failure but in family lore from the heartache of loss. My father was not told of her death when he was in Chicago, for he could not afford the ticket back for her funeral.

My mother is a prolific baker. Before we made our first trip to the United States from our home in Kuwait, we traveled there by way of her delicious apple pies, which celebrated my father's past American life.

My mother spent hours perfecting recipes from her cherished Betty Crocker cookbook. If food is love, then my mother was madly in love. We grew up enjoying American classics: apple pies, lemon meringue pies, cheesecakes, homemade doughnuts, and banana splits.

TWELVE

I Heard It on Hannity

Goodness and evil are not equal. Repel evil with what is fairer.
Then that person with whom there was enmity, may become your
intimate friend!

—Quran 41:34–35

SOME DAYS, AMERICA FEELS OFF-LIMITS TO
Muslims. On those days, it does not seem too keen on its Muslim children. Its promise and grace are compromised by an industry specializing in churning out manufactured fear—a prolific fear that can accost you while picking up a carton of milk from the grocery store, as you catch sight of the angry bearded men staring at you from the cover of a magazine captioned "Muslim Rage: How I Survived It. How We Can End It." It can catch you off guard when you finally decide to open the emails you have deliberately been trying to ignore while on vacation.

One such email I received, which promised to deliver "Islam in a Nutshell," was forwarded to me by Priscilla, who, in the spirit of the Faith Club's commitment to open and honest dialog, felt compelled to share.

"Hi Ranya," she wrote,

I hope you are well. I've been in bed for two weeks with the flu/bronchitis. Was just starting to feel better when I got this email from an old friend . . . oy. Feel free to ignore it, give me your reaction to it, which I will cite to my friend, or use it to inspire your new writing. Let me know your thoughts, as I'd like to respond to her coherently . . .

Love,

P

I have since received two other similar emails, all denigrating Islam in some manner or form and urging the receiver to forward the message to as many people as possible, lest the "truth" remain untold and they end up being a part of the problem. The email Priscilla sent me started out by referencing the work of a Dr. Peter Hammond, an author and "expert on Islam," presumably to lend academic credibility to its explosive claims. Buried under lists of a country-by-country analysis of Muslim population statistics meant to show how Muslims' rising birthrates and religious beliefs prove that Muslims are agitating to take over the world is the following insight:

Maybe this is why American Muslims are so quiet and not speaking out about atrocities. Can a good Muslim be a good American?

Theologically—no. Because his allegiance is to Allah, The moon God of Arabia.

It went on to say how Muslims cannot be good Americans religiously, spiritually, geographically, politically, socially, domestically, and intellectually, and concluded,

Therefore, after much study and deliberation . . . Perhaps we should be very suspicious of ALL MUSLIMS in this country—They obviously cannot be both good Muslims and good Americans.

And so, on a beautiful sunny spring day, out West in the quintessential American landscape—the Rocky Mountains of Colorado—at a little after eight o'clock in the morning, as my children bundled up in their colorful ski layers and drank their hot chocolate, I was called on to coherently defend how my children can indeed be "good" Muslims and "good" Americans. For what it's worth, this is what I wrote back at the time:

Hi P—
We are in Vail skiing. Just opened this and it gave me a stomachache. It's vitriol is all it is. . . . The equivalent of saying

all Jews control all money sources, are scheming greedy thieves who worship money, not God, and don't believe in Jesus and the Bible so how can they pledge allegiance to the U.S. and its Constitution when they all have loyalty to Israel? (Sorry—it is so ugly I am not sure how one can respond to pure hate) I suppose one can try love. . . . xo

Her response:

I pity the poor man who wrote the email. That's a lot of hate, paranoia and anger to live with . . . exhausting! Thought it might spur some writing for you, but feel free to ignore and HAVE FUN IN VAIL! XOXO Priscilla

But the problem is too serious to pity the man for his hate, as much as I would like to not take him seriously, to rationalize away his prejudice. I cannot help but feel that this is perhaps more sinister than just one individual expressing his opinion. It is difficult not to feel persecuted when his feelings and narrative are fed and nourished by a virulent anti-Muslim industry that has a ravenous appetite and spins the legitimate insecurities and wounds of 9/11 into frenzied fear of all things Muslim. Organizations and think tanks with ominous-sounding names such as Stop the Islamization of America or the Freedom Defense Initiative (defending freedom from Muslims) abound. These, along with opaquely financed funds, invest a lot of money, time, and energy in perpetuating an existential—even apocalyptic—fear of Muslims.

We have been there before. We have seen how unchecked hatred of Jews led to the Holocaust, how hyperbolized hate led to the death of journalist Daniel Pearl and to the shooting of Malala Yousafzai, a fifteen-year-old Pakistani girl, because she advocated education for women. From the shootings in Norway to the rapes and mass graves in Bosnia, we have seen what hate can do. It is important that we do not become complacent about how villainous the cocktail of fear and hate can become. While freedom of speech is the most sacred of American rights, we would be wise to heed the advice of former secretary of state Hillary Clinton, who, in the aftermath of the violent protests resulting from the YouTube trailer *The Innocence of Muslims*,[1] noted that "violence in response to free speech is unacceptable."[2] That is an absolute truth, but we would also be well served to remember that free speech can also be abused. It can be used to denigrate and inflame. To criticize or condemn the abuse is not to prohibit it. We can be outraged about what is being said and we must disassociate from it as Americans.

Hate speech and inflammatory remarks are especially treacherous for American Muslim mothers, who often navigate these subversive currents on a daily basis. Such remarks are not simply philosophical, pedantic questions. They can have dangerous consequences, affecting our children's ability to make peace with their identities and feel valued as positive members of society.

Why would my assimilation radar be on such high alert? Why did I question Taymor on the crescent and star inked on his wrist? Because American Muslim mothers instinctively know that radicalization in American-born Muslims is not caused by the Quran: rather, it is rooted in alienation, wherein troubled youths embrace a radicalized perspective of the world, enabled and empowered by radicalized readings of the Quran. We understand how important it is that our first-generation children assimilate. We know that there is nothing more ripe for exploitation than the feelings of the isolated, the lonely, and the taunted: the fragile and belittled egos of the young and teenagers who are looking to belong. Radical organizations such as Al-Qaeda know this too. They mine the feelings of the isolated and lonely, the fragile and belittled egos at the service of their political agendas and egomaniacal goals.

Even when minorities hold on to orthodox religious traditions that may set them apart from their more secular adopted countries, they are still looking to belong and for their children to thrive as equal and loyal citizens. Orthodox minority communities, whether Jewish or Muslim or Sikh, still want to be recognized and legally protected as equal citizens. As Muslims, we know that radicalization in our children is not caused by the Quran but is first born of alienation and then empowered and given meaning by radical and violent readings of the Quran. Our job is made harder when even the benign and somewhat entertaining reality show *All-American Muslim* managed to cause a political storm. When the eight-part series aired on TLC, the show that followed the lives of Muslim families in Dearborn, Michigan, became a lightning rod for the tensions of our identities. The Tampa-based Florida Family Association complained to the giant retailer Lowe's about its advertising slot in the show, explaining that they found the program objectionable because it did not accurately depict Muslims as the families featured were not extremists. Lowe's succumbed and pulled the plug on its ads, confirming many American Muslims' fear: that the bottom line is that Muslims cannot be both American and Muslim. If Muslim youth do not develop well-adjusted, assimilated Western Muslim voices, and if they are rejected as suspect and alien, then arbitrary and radicalized Islam and its preachers can captivate. The challenge for many first-generation American Muslims is to find that dignity and their voice in society in a well-adjusted, productive way. America, should it choose not to enable such a voice, should at the very least try not to hinder its development; but America has not made up its mind.

It is an America that is full of hope and promise, audacious in its ideals, that is our American dream. The one we intuitively choose every step of the way. Even as we considered schools for our children, I knew that even though my husband would have liked them to attend a French school because of the advantages of fluency in many languages, I did not want them immersed in French history and culture. I wanted them to fall in love with our Founding Fathers, as I had, even if it meant forgoing the advantages of fluency in another language. When we were interviewed as part of Leia's admission process for kindergarten, I was always keen to stress our permanence. We were American, here to stay. While the admissions committee was eager to embrace Leia's diversity, I wanted her to be as American as can be. Yet, even a family as secular as ours, that carries no outward symbols of religiosity or clear ethnicity, has had a number of bumps along the way. I see Taymor's feelings of otherness revealed when on vacation he is asked by his freshly minted friend from California where he is from: instead of saying New York, he delves into an explanation of his parents' national roots. I see it in the complexity rendered on the simplest of choices, such as when he bowed his head during his school's Friday morning assembly prayers, and some of the boys questioned him on why a Muslim would make that choice. I see it in the courage it takes for him to laugh along with good friends even as they tease and ask, "Are you attending your leader's [Osama bin Laden's] funeral?" I see it as he tries to make peace with the pulls and pushes of his identity, as he tries to resolve the confusing and complex emotions and the inevitable subliminal Muslim guilt. In a show of self-flagellation, Catholic in proportion, he is earnest when he shares his new resolution: "Since tomorrow is the anniversary of 9/11, I've told my friends that tomorrow at the lunch table they can say anything they want about Muslims. They get a free pass."

This November, I plan to get him a different type of pass. One that will hopefully help with some of the insecurities and doubts he has about his place in America. Every Thanksgiving, we journey down south to share the holiday with my aunt who lives in Virginia. This November, I have planned a trip to the Library of Congress and the Supreme Court, where I cannot wait to share with my children what I have only recently learned. The Library of Congress's main reading room, built in 1897, has a dome with a celestial mural of twelve figures, male and female, who represent the twelve civilizations believed to have contributed the most to modern civilization and to America. These include Egypt for Written Records, Judea for Religion, Greece for Philosophy, Rome for Administration, the Middle Ages for Modern Languages, Italy for Fine Art, Germany for the Art of Printing, Spain for Discovery, England for Literature, France for Emancipation, America for Science, and Islam for Physics. Even more poignant will be a viewing of the stone friezes found on the walls of the chamber in the Supreme Court building. The friezes pay tribute to eighteen lawgivers who have inspired American values and justice. Somewhere between Justinian and John Marshall there is a sculpture of the Prophet Muhammad, Quran and sword (symbolizing the defense of justice) in hand. I wonder what Hannity and friends would have to say about that?

THIRTEEN

"No Muslim Parking"

Let not hatred of others to you make you swerve to wrong and
depart from justice. Be just: that is next to Piety.

—Quran 5:8

COLIN POWELL WAS TOO AMBITIOUS WHEN HE
questioned what would be wrong with a seven-year-old American
Muslim dreaming of becoming president. If you happen to be a
child who is both an American and a Muslim, it is not only presidential dreams that can be curtailed: future athletes and scholars
should also be mindful. If you are like Oday Aboushi, an American and a practicing Muslim who is also proud of his Palestinian
heritage, your identity may make you suspect as a Muslim extremist and anti-Semite. This twenty-first-century Muslim Jackie
Robinson is the Brooklyn-born fifth-round pick of the New York
Jets. No sooner had he rejoiced in his successful professional

career pick than he woke up to a hailstorm of fury and slander, as some wondered if he should be drummed out of the football league. Aboushi was even compared to those who traffic in "anti-gay, anti-black, anti-immigrant, sexist" speech, and the NFL was questioned on its desire to be associated with prejudice, violence, or fundamentalism.[1] All Aboushi had done was talk to a group about how proud he was to be Palestinian and how eager he was to play in the NFL. But his identity was his crime. Jonathan Mael, Major League Baseball's new media coordinator, compared Aboushi to Aaron Hernandez, the Patriots football player who is facing murder charges, when he tweeted: "The Patriots have Aaron Hernandez, the Jets have Oday Aboushi."

And if you happen to be an accomplished and highly quali-fied scholar with a PhD in the sociology of religions, in addition to other graduate and undergraduate degrees including a master's degree in theological studies from the Harvard Divinity School, and you end up writing a book about the historical Jesus, it is best if you are not a Muslim. Reza Aslan has learned this. His interview on Fox made for gruesomely uncomfortable viewing, as his inter-viewer relentlessly and for eight long television minutes refused to move beyond the incredulous idea that a Muslim, who is a gifted and erudite scholar with multiple degrees in religion, could possi-bly write a scholarly book about Jesus without having a hidden and nefarious Muslim agenda. Reza maintained his calm demeanor as Lauren Green of Fox drilled him on his concealed and true mo-tives as a Muslim writing on Jesus: "You're a Muslim, so why did you write a book about the founder of Christianity?" At one point she even brazenly and bizarrely accused him of having concealed his identity as a Muslim, forcing Reza to remind her that he is a well-known and prolific author who has always been transparent about his faith, which he even mentions on the second page of the book in question. To appreciate the degree of suspicion, contempt, and derision toward all things Muslim that forms the basis of such logic, imagine if a scholar who happens to be Christian, Jewish, or atheist were to be questioned on his secret motives for writing about his chosen field of expertise. We would not have many Fox-sanctioned legitimate academic books left on our shelves. As Reza pointed out, Christian or Jewish scholars write most of the scholarly books about Islam in America, and no one has ever thought to question them about their true and undeclared motives.

In America today, Muslims are the only minority about whom mainstream public figures, journalists, politicians, and academics can make outlandish, outright racist, xenophobic remarks and continue as respected, credible public figures; in some quarters, making those remarks can actually further one's career. That is the world in which my children are coming of age. A world where otherwise highly intelligent and highly educated people can make the most unintelligent remarks about Muslims. New Atheist Richard Dawkins believes that you can have an opinion about Islam without reading the Quran because, as he recently tweeted, "you don't have to read Mein Kampf to have an opinion about Nazism." He also tweeted that all the world's Muslims have fewer Nobel Prizes than Trinity College, Cambridge, a statistic whose inferred conclusions do not sit as well with our intellectual sensibilities if we are to replace it with another equally valid statistic: that all the world's blacks have fewer Nobel Prizes than Trinity College, Cambridge.[2] Fellow New Atheist Sam Harris is a proponent of religious profiling: "We should profile Muslims, or anyone who looks like he could conceivably be Muslim."[3] I wonder if he would be just as comfortable saying that we should profile all blacks, Mexicans, Catholics, Jews, or anyone who looks like he could conceivably be black, Mexican, Catholic, or Jewish. In a litmus test of true American values and patriotism, mainstream presidential candidates and politicians such as Republican Herman Cain promised to never consider appointing a Muslim to his administration. Replace that with the promise of never appointing a woman or an Asian American or a Jew to appreciate the audacity of the prejudice and discrimination it assumes. If you are still not convinced, maybe former representative Allen West of Florida will sway you. He claimed that Muslims are naturally wild because God cursed Ishmael and his descendants. According to Pat Robertson, a former Southern Baptist minister and media tycoon, Muslims are like Hitler, and Americans should fight Islam as they fought Nazi Germany.

If these outspoken media fixtures are to be believed, Muslims cannot be loyal Americans because they cannot truthfully swear the oath and be bound to the Constitution, which is superseded by their loyalty to the Quran. They are engaged in a jihad that uses America's tolerance for freedom of religion to build mosques and wage holy war against all Christians and Jews as mandated by their God and their religion. They are a duplicitous fifth column, looking to take over the White House and impose Sharia law on innocent, unsuspecting, naive liberal Americans. No matter how much Muslims protest against such allegations, or try to defend themselves, it is a futile effort. Americans are advised not to believe them, because naturally, Muslims' religion mandates that they should lie in order to further their objectives. It is not that other minorities do not suffer from racist slurs, slander, or stereotypes. They most certainly do. The pivotal difference is that when such epithets are made about other minority groups, there are often consequences. At the very least, there is outrage by some and a predominant visceral understanding that such gross generalizations are nothing but vitriol and hateful speech. When it comes to Muslims, however, such vitriol is not exclusive to the few, the fringe, or the peripheral. It is public, mainstream, and believed by otherwise intelligent and lovely people. If Fox News is a benchmark for such persuasions, then it is America's truth for many in our nation. When such vitriol becomes so commonplace, our senses are lulled into believing that a "No Muslim Parking" sign posted near a Texas mall adjacent to a mosque could possibly be anything but offensive.[4] Again, a good litmus test for our dulled Muslim sensibilities is to replace Muslim with any other religion: try "No Jewish Parking."

Politicians such as Mike Huckabee represent the frustrations of those Americans who feel unfairly edited into silence because of notions of political correctness. He recently voiced such complaints: "I know we're not supposed to say anything unkind about Islam." He continued:

> I mean, it's politically incorrect. I get that. But can someone explain to me why it is that we tiptoe around a religion that promotes the most murderous mayhem on the planet in their so-called "holiest days." . . . So the Muslims will go to the Mosque, and they will have their day of prayer, and they come out like uncorked animals. . . . Now, my point is—I mean do you ever say "Oh boy, it's Christmas! Oh my gosh, these Christians are going to come out of that Christmas Eve service and they are going to Wal-Mart, and they are going to so rip that place apart, because you know what happens when they go in there and pray about Jesus. And they get out of there and they go straight to the mall, and they just, I mean they set fire to the place."[5]

I like to think that as a family we are not too indulgent. That we do not wallow in self-pity and victimhood. We have even lived through days when we have felt that the vitriol and hate are deserved and well earned, a human and natural consequence of the Boston Marathon bombings or of the debased and lunatic lone actions of deranged individuals who use their angst and political convictions to justify the beheading of a British soldier or a massacre at Fort Hood. We wonder through the shame and horror if that gracious line extended by those who refuse to vilify and fear will finally break—or whether it even deserves to break. Our identity is precariously perched at the mercy of the next act of terror, which will cast us as either victims or criminals by association. But Mr. Huckabee would be well served to remember that it would not have taken much for him not to inflame the anger, fear, and racism that have become the reality of many Americans who look for him to lead. All he would have to do is not change his opinion, but rather qualify it to point out that it is not the orthodox, or standard, or accepted belief of the overwhelming majority of the 1.6 billion Muslims around the world. Rather, it is perhaps the belief of the radicalized and violent few. All Mr. Huckabee would have to say is that as Americans we will not tiptoe around those Muslims who *choose* to be violent or who promote mayhem. He could even say that there are *some* Muslims who become "uncorked animals," as unsavory as the image may be. But that is how bigotry works; blacks and Jews know that only too well. One takes a group, a minority in one's midst, and recasts them as a collective: a group without individual beliefs, traits, qualities, personalities, emotions, and tendencies. They are stripped of their individuality, their personalities, worries and woes, dreams and desires. This effectively strips them of their humanity. Once they are stripped of humanity, no crime or hate or allegation seems too far-fetched or inconceivable. One can lynch or mob or raze—all while occupying a perceived higher moral ground and a notion of higher civility, intellect, and morality. This is not just un-American: it is un-human. As Americans, we expect and deserve more from our leaders and public figures.

FOURTEEN

"Mom, Are All Terrorists Muslims?"

The ink of a scholar is holier than the blood of a martyr.

—Hadith

TAYMOR WAS ONLY SEVEN YEARS OLD WHEN he confessed that bearded men who look Muslim make him nervous and then asked, "Are all terrorists Muslims?" Who can blame him? On some days, it certainly feels that way. I wish I could say that I was shocked by his question or that he was the first to think that thought. Seven years on, at school his peers insist that the cliché "Not every Muslim is a terrorist, but every terrorist is a Muslim" is true. Stereotypes about Islam abound, but perhaps there is none more insidious and more difficult to disarm than the idea that Islam is at its heart a violent religion. No matter the statistics, and in spite of the 1.6 billion Muslims around the world who live peaceful, charitable, and virtuous lives—which, they believe, are inspired by their faith—the West remains skeptical. This skepticism was vividly and painfully confirmed on 9/11, even if it was not born on that day. For centuries, boorish Muslim violence has been a perennial staple motif in Western art and literature, and it has found more current popular expression in accessible blockbuster Hollywood productions. To be fair, the current belief in Islam's inherent violence is not only the West's burden to bear. Muslims must consider and reflect on the causes that continue to make them vulnerable to such claims. The Arab Spring notwithstanding, far too many Muslims live in states that have yet to establish peaceful and pluralistic systems of governance. As Americans we have long-secured guarantees that protect the freedom of our press and of our speech. America is built on traditions that have successfully integrated the diverse, the different, and the new. Every four years for over two hundred years, Americans have been guaranteed the peaceful transfer of power from president to president. In contrast, many Muslim majority countries have yet to pacify and regulate their political processes. This has left Muslims vulnerable to anarchists and nihilists and illegitimate dictatorships that, lacking a legitimate mandate from the people, will revert to a "mandate from God" and will use anything and everything to remain in power, including, and most importantly, Islam. In the absence of credible and legitimate political institutions, God is a powerful force to invoke for self-serving absolute leaders and their staunch opposition and detractors. Instead of man being in the service of God, far too often in today's Muslim hands, God is in the service of man.

The result is that no other faith tradition suffers from such a radical "perception gap" between its faithful and its detractors and critics. Those who are on the inside insist that Islam is a religion of peace, and those on the outside are absolutely sure that Islam is a religion of violence. The dichotomy between how the majority of Muslims understand and explain their faith and how many in the West do is ever widening and now includes growing concern about "homegrown terrorism." The criminalization of all things Muslim on one hand and the reactionary sanctification and idealization of Islam on the other is expanding in the popular imagination. I watched, disheartened, as the audience of an Intelligence Squared debate—sponsored by NPR and open to the public, who buy tickets to attend—voted in favor of the team that argued that Islam is indeed a violent religion. The conviction that within the tenets, traditions, scripture, and history of Islam lie the roots and inspiration for the violence and terror committed in its name today is a truism for many in the West. The Prophet of Islam, Muhammad, is seen first and foremost as a warrior: Islam's Constantine, who spread the faith by the sword. His role is compared unfavorably to that of Jesus, who embodied love and who walked voluntarily to his death.

The belief in the inherent violence of Islam is not confined to extremists such as Steven Klein, the American veteran who became the spokesperson for the YouTube trailer *The Innocence of Muslims*. When asked if he felt any remorse about the violence that ensued, he explained that he did not because he did not create the violence; it was already inside Muslims. The belief that Muslims are more violent than Christians or Jews or Buddhists is not limited to extremists, and it has become a mainstream idea. It is even being taught in my son's history book as a historical fact and promises to be an even bigger challenge with a future generation of Americans.

When Taymor was in fifth grade, he came home frustrated one day. His history textbook explained that Muslims believe in a God called "Allah," as if Allah were some exotic, exclusively Muslim deity without any connections to Christianity and Judaism. "That's not true, is it?" he wanted to know. Later on that evening, I walked into his room as he was finishing his history reading assignment. I could see he was distressed, but I was not ready for what came next. "Mom, how can we be Muslims? It says here Muslims are supposed to kill the unbelievers." My heart sank to my knees at the thought of what millions of American children were being taught as conventional Muslim practice. I read the offensive line, hoping against hope that he had misunderstood—but to no avail. The myth is so pervasive in the American psyche that the author of this middle school–friendly history book, *The Story of the World: History for the Classical Child*, inserted between quotation marks what she claims is the text, verbatim, of the Quran or the words of the Prophet: "'Only Muslims will be allowed to enter

Mecca from this day on,' Muhammad declared. 'Any unbelievers who enter will be put death!'"[1] The quotations are the author's, not mine. There is no footnote or reference to her source. I have consulted numerous Imams and scholars and no one can authenticate her claim. In other words, no one I know can find those words in the Quran or in the Hadith (the Prophet's sayings).

Even Diane Sawyer may have been swayed by the belief that Islam is by definition a violent religion. As I was being interviewed for a special *20/20* feature on Islam, she asked me to explain how, although Jews had suffered centuries of discrimination and persecution in the West, unlike Muslims, they had not turned to violence and terrorism. The assumption here is that unlike Jewish or other minorities, there is something inherently violent about Muslims, that Islam as a religion is more prone to churning out terror and terrorists. At face value it seems rather convincing. After all, Jews suffered years of persecution in Europe without developing into homegrown terrorists. The difference is this: There was no Jewish state that was at war with or was occupied by the European Jews' native European home state, as is the case for European and American Iraqis and Afghans. Nor was there a recent memory of violent imperial conquests and humiliating colonial grievances perpetrated by any European Jews' country of citizenship against a Jewish state. There was no perception that Christian or Western imperialists were supporting loathed Jewish dictators in return for Jewish oil. Many Muslims, on the other hand, see themselves as victims of European and Western aggression. Al-Qaeda has successfully harnessed that political narrative to pursue its violent and maniacal objectives. Western Jews experiencing discrimination and problems of assimilation did not have, as Muslims do, a militant geopolitical global movement such as Al-Qaeda, which has made it its mission to actively recruit the disenfranchised and the less than stable to seek redemption and avenge perceived injustices through a call to arms ordained by God. Jewish suffering was not turned into an Al-Qaeda style paramilitary movement of terror because their political and historical circumstances were very different. That is, until the emergence of Zionism, which, when it finally met British colonial resistance to its goal of establishing a Jewish homeland in British-occupied Palestine, produced its own version of Jewish terrorism and paramilitary forces: the Irgun and the Stern Gang. The perceived legitimacy of "the cause"—the creation of a Jewish homeland, or resisting perceived Western injustices in the case of Muslims—is used to justify the violent means. The obvious conclusion is that it is not Judaism or Islam that is responsible for active violence but rather a politicized and militarized Jewish or Muslim narrative, inflamed by real territorial or political conflicts, confirmed by local experiences of perceived or real grievances that then become a call for violent action.

The West's belief in the violence of Islam has created a reactionary and defensive position on the part of many Muslims. They insist on repeating the mantra that Islam is a religion of peace, which is a counterproductive, ineffective and futile approach. The question of whether Islam is a religion of peace is by definition polarizing and puts Muslims on the defensive. American Muslim hypersensitivity to the allegations that Islam is a religion of the sword has even made them object to Muhammad's presence on the frieze in the Supreme Court chamber, afraid that the sword reinforces the very stereotypes that they are desperate to shed. They defensively look back to Muslim rule in Spain, dubbed the "ornament of the world" by María Rosa Menocal,[2] and celebrate the diversity and pluralism that were embraced by Muslim rule as the ideals that are the true embodiment of its message. I do not doubt the sincerity of this belief; 1.6 billion Muslims have not taken up arms and are not jihadis who are looking to smite the necks of the infidels. Cherry-picking verses as proof of the inevitable violence of Islam and Muslims is insincere and disingenuous. It is a position that allies itself with the violent in opposition to the majority of Muslims who insist otherwise. It only serves to strengthen the hands of Muslims who are violent by validating their violent readings of scripture and glorifying and legitimizing their cause by acquiescing to their logic and interpretations. It is a better strategy to believe and affirm the convictions of the overwhelming majority of Muslims, who absolutely reject those verses as a mandate for violence and look to analyze and understand them in a limited and contained historical context.

Muslims, however, would also be better served by acknowledging that while no religion is immune to being used to justify violence, Islam today is more vulnerable than other religions; that Islam is living a violent moment in its history because it finds itself in the crosscurrents of violent change in countries experiencing tumultuous civic, cultural, and political transitions. Islam today is at war with itself. It is in a more rudimentary stage politically, socially, and institutionally, making it vulnerable to the vanities of human ambition and violence. We would be well served as Muslims to apply ourselves to protecting Islam from such vulnerabilities. All religions have within them the capacity for war and for peace. For this reason, when a friend suggests that I should publish under a pseudonym, I do not think she is being absurd because the sad reality is that many Muslim and non-Muslim voices have been threatened with violence. Those who are interested in rooting for advocates of a peaceful, pluralistic Islam should not be denying its very possibility. To ask the question "Is Islam a religion of peace or is Islam a religion of violence or war?" is a futile and even silly exercise. Islam is as violent or as peaceful as the Muslim believer wills it to be. Since overwhelming numbers of Muslims have not taken up arms and are not jihadis against Christians, Jews, and non-believers, it is safe to conclude that the overwhelming majority of Muslims are peaceful and believe in a peaceful Islam.

Radicalization is not exclusive to Muslims. To my son and all those who still insist otherwise: no, not all terrorists are Muslims. Sadly, we have examples of fundamentalist Christian extremists killing doctors who perform abortions in the name of saving lives. We have Jewish extremists who have gunned down politicians they disagree with and who they feel are not safeguarding Jewish interests in Jewish lands given to them through the promise of God. We have had Hindus and Sikhs and most recently Buddhists engaging in violence in the name of their religions. The contradictions of our human minds are baffling and worrisome. But they are sadly not unique or exceptional to Muslims. We would all be better Muslims, Christians, Jews, Sikhs, Hindus, and Buddhists if we recognize that within our faiths lies the possibility of both war and peace and dedicate ourselves to securing the peace.

FIFTEEN

The Path to the
Watering Hole

*Let there be no compulsion [or coercion] in the religion [Islam]. The
right direction is distinctly clear from error.*

—Quran 2:256

"HOW DO YOU FEEL ABOUT THE THREAT OF
Sharia [Islamic law] in America?" I was asked at the end of a
Q&A session in South Carolina. As a speaker, I always try to
prepare for the tough questions. I had the "Smite their neck" and
the "kill the infidel!" verses covered: "Those verses were limited
to those specific conditions and are to be understood only in their
relevant historical context," I explained to my audiences. "They
were certainly not a wholesale excuse for murder." Besides, "infidel" is a Christian word and does not refer to Christians or Jews,

for, as any grade school Muslim will tell you, Christians and Jews are revered as "People of the Book." A cardinal tenet of the faith is the belief that Islam is not a different religion, but rather the continuation of the same revelation that began with Abraham, the father of monotheism, and who is mentioned sixty-nine times in the Quran. Early Islam's connections to Christianity were so discernable that some Christians of the time believed it was a heretical sect of Christianity. A more accurate translation of the Arabic word *kafir* is not "infidel"—which is more of a Christian medieval term used to describe the Saracens or Muslims—but the root of the word "to bury" in Arabic, or "those who bury God's justice and truth." I then proposed to my audiences that the tragic irony of the current state of Judeo-Christian-Muslim affairs is best appreciated when you consider that the Muslim Supreme Collection of Canonic Laws states: "He who believes all that he is bound to believe, except that he says, 'I do not know whether Moses and Jesus (Peace be upon them) do or do not belong to the Messengers,' is an infidel."[1]

I was also prepared for the most insidious of Muslim words: jihad. I explained how I have a favorite uncle, Uncle Jihad. There was a time when it was a popular and common name for boys, like John. In Arabic, its root word can mean "to strive, to labor, to pursue with effort, to struggle against evil in order to live a righteous life." Theologically, the word has two meanings. Muslims believe that the greater jihad is the jihad of the soul. It is a spiritual effort, an internal striving to conquer our sins and control our urges, to resist temptation: to strive toward a closer connection with God as we seek a life of equilibrium and justice in our relationships with others and nature. To control a temper. To resist the creeping cynicism of life. To edit our disdain. To give, to smile, to be kind. To forgive. To accept. To conquer our arrogance and remain in awe of God. To see God in the rising sun, feel him in the daily miracles of life—the birth of a child or a guarded nest of eggs. To have faith that good will prevail. This jihad is not only Muslim: it is Christian, and Jewish, and Buddhist, and more. It is human. It is jihad in search of the love and grace of God. A jihad that I am on every day.

The lesser jihad, the one that has been radicalized by extremists who use it to justify violence, I clarified, was intended to be defensive by definition, neither sought nor encouraged, and never intended to be a holy war of dominion, aggression, and conquest. Nor is it the call to spread Islam by the sword. It is recognition that in the face of extreme oppression, of ethnic cleansing, of genocide, of rape and destruction, military options are sometimes legitimate solutions. It is a study of what constitutes just and unjust wars. The systematic killing of a people because of race, color, or faith; the degradation, rape, enslavement, and deformation of women with acid on the face, a common practice of the Taliban, are arguably cases where violence can be contained only with force. Blowing up planes, placing bombs on buses and trains, is terror, not jihad. Avenging a perceived injustice by killing civilians and innocent bystanders is terror, not jihad.

Life is precious, and Muslims believe "that to take away a human life is to take away the life of humanity, and to save a life is to save humanity."[2] However, even the most committed of pacifists understand that as unsavory as the use of force is, it may be a necessary check on the insatiable human capacity for cruelty. The evil lurking in the shadows of our humanity can and has reigned. Under those conditions, the use of force may be just. Even then, Muslims are asked to honor treaties and not to transgress limits, "for God loves not transgressors. . . . Let there be no hostility except to those who practice oppression."[3]

Although President Obama seems to be having trouble these days convincing some Americans that he is not a Muslim, it was not too long ago that some argued that candidate Obama would be at risk in the Muslim world because he is an apostate (*murtad*) who did not embrace the religion of his father—a crime punishable in Islam by death. This is another classic example of accepting a skewed extremist view as the Muslim norm. Muslims who believe in the death penalty for apostasy are certainly not basing their position on the Quran. In fact, the Quran is full of injunctions against compulsion in religion. Rather, it declares: "To you, your religion and to me, mine."[4] Most importantly, there is not a single verse in the Quran which prescribes capital punishment for apostasy.[5] Although the Quran considers it a great offense, as seen in verse 4:137 ("Behold, as for those who come to believe, and then deny the truth, and again come to believe, and again deny the truth, and thereafter grow stubborn in their denial of truth—God

will not forgive them, nor will guide them in any way"), its punishment is believed to be between man and his creator. Instances
when the Hadith, or the Prophet's oral tradition, is used to justify
capital punishment are not for cases of a simple reversal of faith.
These are better understood in their historical context as apostasy
accompanied by treason and sedition, which would have placed the
Muslim community at fatal risk, more akin to military treason. It is
not a judgment on personal belief or spiritual choice. It is not the
gruesome charade of murder perpetrated in the name of God. To
force someone to remain in a faith they do not believe is absurd,
negating sincere belief and endorsing hypocrisy instead. This is not
Islam.

Finally, I assured my audience that Muslims believe the Quran
needs to be read as a whole, as a complete entity, for its truth to
be fully understood and appreciated. The message of a forgiving
and just God is so much more prevalent. Besides, it is not what
non-Muslims believe or what Western scholars want you to believe that matters most; it is what the overwhelming majority of
Muslims choose to believe that matters most, and they believe
that Islam is a force of good, justice, and well-being in their lives.

The question of Sharia as a threat to America was something
I really had not anticipated. I had lived forty-some years without
feeling threatened by Sharia, most certainly not as an American,
so I was curious about the question. I am fully aware of the corruption and criminal abuse of Sharia law in countries like Afghanistan and Pakistan and Iran, but I was certain that this was

not something I had to fear in America. It seemed redundant to point out to my questioner that America's legal system is secular and protected by the Constitution. All Americans know that the Constitution already makes it illegal to use religious law as the law of the land. We understand the sanctity of our secular court systems. We do not worry that America will be threatened by Christian canon law or Jewish halakah law. Yet here I was, called on to express my feelings on what had clearly become a new chapter in the American Muslim divide.

The "Muslim Scare," similar to other "scares" such as the Red Scare, is not based on rational thoughts but on fear: irrational fear of subversive Muslims' creeping influence on America and its court systems. This fear springs from the belief that without the required appropriate vigilance from "true Americans," American Muslims put at risk—and can eventually take over—America. As the NYPD recruiting video showed, there are those who fear that this may one day result in the Muslim flag flying over the White House. Nowhere is the manufacture of fear so vivid as in the fabricated fear of Sharia in America. The idea that America's court systems are so vulnerable that they risk being taken over by Sharia's influence is absurd and is nothing other than one more front in the demagoguery that Muslims continue to face as they are told that they are lesser citizens or that they cannot be both American and Muslim.

Yet, there are those who deny the existence of Islamophobia. They protest that to disagree with the central tenets of the faith or to criticize Muslims is not to be an Islamophobe. Besides, they add, since Muslims are not one ethnicity, their experiences cannot be akin to the Jewish experience of anti-Semitism. For all those who do not see or recognize the problem, just speak to any American Muslim kid. I will start with mine. The terrorist jokes, the references to bombs and hidden weapons caches, are thinly veiled feelings of contempt for our religion. A contempt that seeps through to affect what should be the most benign of choices and decisions: as the Islamophobic narrative has become more prevalent, its distilled perniciousness has permeated our lives so that a simple school tradition has given us reason to pause. As the boys graduate from middle school, they are given the opportunity to design and carve wooden plaques commemorating their years as students of the school. These then adorn the walls of the school for posterity. The themes have been wide and varied, and often include their names, the number of years at the school, and personal emblems or motifs, from hockey sticks to music notes to peace signs. Taymor wanted to include two elements he felt are important to his identity: the crescent and the star, and an American flag. Over dinner he took pencil to paper as he considered possible designs. As a way of integrating them he thought he would place the Muslim symbol on the flag. As he sketched a version of the American flag with crescent and stars in the upper left-hand corner, I immediately gasped and vetoed the idea. Suddenly I was horrified, as the image that I had dismissed as too inflammatory to believe, the White House with a

Muslim flag on top, was resonating ominously in the sketch he had produced in our kitchen. I explained to Taymor that some Americans are convinced of a covert Muslim plot to take over America and infiltrate its institutions, and that the symbol of Islam juxtaposed on the American flag would make many people feel uncomfortable. He finally settled on just a crescent and a star, with no flag, but even that puzzled his classmates, who asked, "Do you even go to mosque?" I wondered if that would have been the reaction to a Star of David or to a cross. The contempt is real. It is not imagined. Maybe it is deserved. But it is not invented.

I feel America's fear. I really do. The only way that Islamophobia can get any traction is because it plays on people's genuine fears. Some days I too feel that fear. I also feel America's contempt. I watch *Fox and Friends*, visit Jihad Watch, and try to understand. I imagine that I am not Muslim, that I do not know any Muslims. I imagine that I believe that Muslims are out to kill the infidels, to smite their necks; that Christians and Jews are the enemies of Islam; that Muslims have always celebrated their military victories by building mosques on top of churches and temples; that there is no such thing as a moderate Muslim. It is an oxymoron. I imagine that I believe that there should be an Islamofascism awareness week on college campuses; that Islam is inherently violent, a religion of the sword spread by the sword, seeking world dominion; that Muhammad is a false prophet, a thief, a rapist, an assassin, a pedophile; that Islam hates us for our freedoms, for our values, and that Islam is anti-democracy and pro-theocracy and therefore a threat to our security.

This fear is reinforced and infused with shame when I read how Indonesian Muslims featured in a *National Geographic* article have to face fanatics in Aceh Province who have produced a pamphlet on Sharia law that reads like a torture manual from the Middle Ages: "If you're caught gambling: six to twelve lashes. Improperly mingling with the opposite sex: three to nine lashes. Drinking alcohol: forty lashes. Skipping prayer on three consecutive Fridays: three lashes."[6] In case readers missed the point, there was a photo album of the more than one hundred whippings that have taken place since 2005. No detail was left unattended. A photo of the hooded "master" flogger donning a maroon robe and white gloves was included along with the required specifications of the instrument of torture: it must be made of rattan and at least a quarter of an inch thick.

In the very name "Sharia" lies the key to our salvation and what many Muslims have forgotten. Sharia, the name given to the body of Islamic law, literally means "the path to the watering hole." The "Miracle of Zamzam" is the watering hole delivered by God to save Hagar and Ishmael after their abandonment by Abraham in the desert. Hagar and Ishmael were left to languish in the desert, but God did not forsake them. In the parched, scorching heat of the desert, water was their salvation, the enabler of life. Sharia, or the path to the watering hole, is the path to God—the sustainer of life, the savior of souls. It is the mercy of God. Pilgrims to Mecca visit Zamzam and carry back home its holy water, as my mother did, to bless and protect loved ones. For we are all in search of salvation as we pray that God will not forsake us and that our souls will be quenched with righteousness so that we too are delivered the paths to our watering holes. Today the path to God seems so far removed from that poetry. When you think of Sharia law, you do not think of watering holes. You think of caged women behind convoluted, torturous shrouds, stripped of their humanity, honor, and dignity. You think of self-appointed vigilantes and soldiers of God flogging, stoning, and amputating. You think of the path to hell.

With the Arab Spring and the youth movements sweeping much of the Muslim world, there is an increasing awareness and passionate desire to put an end to the mockery that masquerades as Sharia justice. The Internet is increasingly congested with new, vibrant, and passionate Muslim voices who are speaking up. Who promise to deliver on the work of progressive scholars such as Fazlur Rahman, a Pakistani American who lectured at the University of Chicago until his death in 1988. He warned of the dangers of reading the Quran as if it were a legal, technical manual prescribing what "should" or "should not" be done. He argued against making the Quran ahistorical and insisted that "revelation" cannot function outside history. He believed that the Quran should be read as a moral and ethical text based on *taqwa,* or God's consciousness. Laws should not be rigid but should reflect the vibrancy and flexibility of Islam in its different historical contexts and centuries. Sharia is a dynamic and changing human effort to understand what is fully known only to God. Floggings in Sudan, amputations in Somalia, lashings in Saudi Arabia are not what Muslims want Sharia to be. There are no excuses for those who use blasphemy laws to punish a Christian girl in Pakistan or to shoot a Muslim girl for advocating education for girls. Those who have made Sharia into an obsolete punitive system obsessed with regulating people's vices as opposed to a true quest for justice or *taqwa* are criminals. They have failed in their moral obligations, not only as Muslims but as humans.

Fear is not the American way, I remind my children. So although I feel America's fear, and on some days even share its contempt or disdain, I do not believe that doing so reflects America at its best. As we strive for a better American union, it is knowledge and compassion, rather than fear mongering and ignorance, that must reign supreme. Today more than ever, America's hope, vision, and exceptionalism are needed as an inspiration for those who are aspiring and struggling to gain the freedoms and rights we already have. Banning imagined threats such as Sharia in an America that has had centuries of safeguarded and absolutely secular courts only serves to infringe on the equality and rights of Muslims as Americans, making them feel targeted and persecuted. It reflects a less than honest America, lacking in confidence, insecure in its mission. Let our conviction not be fear but knowledge and power—this has always been the American way. As a confident America moves forward in its expansive power of assimilation, I hope that my children too are a part of that larger and better union, a stronger union, and a union that includes American Muslims. Let us inspire Muslims all over the world as they pursue a justice and a freedom that we as Americans have long known.

SIXTEEN

"Mommy, Can I Marry a Jew?"

And verily we gave the Children of Israel the Scripture, and the Command, and Prophethood; and provided them with good things and favored them above (all) peoples.

—Quran 45:16

MY MOTHER, A PALESTINIAN REFUGEE, WOULD say to me when I was too young to appreciate how radical she sounded, "Whoever you end up falling in love with, you can marry, even if he is Jewish." The "even if he is Jewish" in the context of her personal experiences was an expression of her unconditional love, her way of saying, "I will love you no matter what," even if you do what is considered unimaginable for a Palestinian family who suffered loss and heartache as a result of the Jewish state of Israel. Maybe she had the courage to say it because it was all so theoretical. After all, there were no Jewish boys in Dubai for me to love. Or maybe she was a hopeless romantic. Either way, I found her position curious but empowering; even if it seemed too far removed from my immediate teen concerns and crushes to be relevant. But when my daughter, who had spent the better part of her thirteenth year attending bar mitzvah and bat mitzvah celebrations in New York City, asked me, "Mommy, can I marry a Jew?" I had every reason to pause. She knew more Jewish boys than Muslim boys. She had been to more temples and churches than mosques. The unimaginable was now a tangible, maybe even a probable. I wish I could say that I did not have to stop for a moment and think. I know I am not alone. When I was still traveling as part of an extended book tour for *The Faith Club*, I had more than a few distressed mothers share their anxieties. In the case of at least one, there was panic about her Jewish son's Muslim bride: "She refuses to bring the children up as Jewish," she agonized. Why do many parents loathe the prospects of interfaith marriages? Or as one Jewish mother put it, "I tell my children not to go there. It is a red line; they should just not allow themselves to fall in love with a non-Jew."

Her position may sound extreme, but it is probably closer to the truth than many of us would care to admit. The truth of the matter is that most of us are ambivalent about interfaith marriages, if not passionately averse to them. Marriage is the ultimate identity question. Whom you marry, where you marry, how you marry, define the family you choose to become as you leave the family you were randomly assigned at birth. Choices that stray from the cultural and religious identities of our parents make what is under normal circumstances a challenging process even more difficult. Children and grandchildren are about our perpetuity; they promise us life after death. They are how we will be remembered. Whom we marry, and where and how we marry, tells our stories. Whether it is in the way we set the table or hand down recipes or the way we worship. They are our personal histories and an affirmation of our communal yearnings. Through our children and grandchildren we are renewing our membership in our communities. Whether in the tradition of decorating a tree or lighting the menorah candles or the flavors of the feast after our fasts, there is great joy in sharing and honoring our rituals and memories. No wonder parents have such strong feelings about the identity of their children's prospective spouses. Psychological studies have shown that even babies have shown an innate preference for those whom they perceive as most similar to them in personal taste and choice. Biologically, we may be hardwired to prefer that our children marry people who are of similar religious backgrounds and ethnicities. The 1967 film *Guess Who's Coming to Dinner* memorialized the racial tensions of interracial marriages, which were outright illegal in certain states as recently as the 1960s. I have uncomfortable visions of Leia being the latest American manifestation of *Guess Who's Coming to Dinner* as she is introduced as the "Muslim girlfriend." What would her beau say to appease his parents? "Oh, she is not really religious. No, she does not pray five times a day. Don't worry, she is not like what you think Muslims are like."

Every religious tradition has its own marriage rituals and cultural expectations. We want to belong and to be recognized and celebrated by our chosen religious communities, not dismissed or shunned. Interfaith marriages threaten that and more. In more conservative cultures, unsanctioned marriage choices are seen as compromising the family's honor and social standing. Difficult as it may seem to us as Americans, who have flourished as a melting pot of races and ethnicities, unsanctioned marriage choices can be life threatening in some countries. While the consequences are not as dire for most, even with the most benign inclinations they still force us out of our comfort zones as we become more conscious of the religious presumptions and stereotypes we hold toward each other. The Jewish identity has been beleaguered and persecuted for so long that there is a sense of responsibility and pride in marrying from within. There is also a strong tribal, ethnic component to Judaism that becomes important when one is thinking of children and grandchildren. If a religion is defined through membership in a tribe or a bloodline, it is easy to see how marriage to my Muslim daughter, who is outside that bloodline, would feel threatening. For more conservative Christians, Leia as a bride might present reason for concern since she has not accepted Jesus as her savior, thereby precluding her place and her children's places in God's heavenly kingdom. Traditionally, Muslims have taken a patriarchal approach to interfaith marriages. Many may be surprised to learn that Muslim men can marry a Jewish or Christian woman without requiring the wife to convert. The underlying assumption is that the children will take on the father's religion. Muslim women (sorry, Leia) have not enjoyed that privilege, and many a man in the name of love has uttered the *shahada*, or declaration of faith: "I bear witness that there is no god but God, and I bear witness that Muhammad is a messenger of God," as a prerequisite for marriage. Progressive Muslims believe that the assumption that men can dictate the religion of the house is faulty and untrue in our non-tribal, beyond-the-seventh-century world, arguing that this interfaith marriage right should also be extended to women.

Leia and Taymor, should you be so magnanimous as to consider my feelings when it is time for you to make your personal choices, here is what I think. My ambivalence about interfaith marriages does not extend to conversion. I have met many women who have chosen either to convert or to bring up their children completely in the faith of the father or perhaps the other way. I respect their choice but hope it will not be yours. If conversion becomes a prerequisite for marriage, I worry that you are not entering a marriage on an equal footing, that one partner's identity is more important than the other's. In view of the feeling that Islam is a beleaguered identity or at the very least challenged, I feel that we owe it to remain true to it. You will be told that conversion is necessary so that children may not grow up confused. That your children's hybrid religious identities will make them feel not Jewish or Muslim or Christian enough. Your children, you will be told, will have to choose one religion over the other, or one parent has to defer to the other. Your children will be made to feel less than authentic, qualifying for neither. Some may advise you to introduce both religions and accept that the children will choose one over the other when they are old enough. As I discussed interfaith marriages with my aunt, trying to sort out my feelings, I explained to her that although I was not sure about interfaith marriages, I was certain that I was not for conversion. I was of the point of view that there is truth in all religions. "Why can't they be both?" I asked. "The children can't be both Jewish and Muslim," my aunt dismissively insisted.

And suddenly it dawned on me. For far too many, being of one religion is about rejecting the other's truth, about one truth trumping all other truths. Or about being saved, chosen, or favored in paradise. A friend recently took those swab tests advertised by *National Geographic* that can trace your DNA and break it down to trace all the ancestral components it may carry. Most of us have accepted that we are not of one ethnic race; we are weary of the supremacist undertones of those who speak of a purity of a race. We accept—I personally would be excited and thrilled to discover—that there may be the unexpected and unknown African or Native American or Asian in the mystery of my ancestors' DNA. Why then do we still look for purity in religions? Religions in their rituals, rules, traditions, and cultures are but expressions; human expressions, flawed expressions, of a common universal yearning, embedded in the beginning of human time, our search for the meaning of life, the search for God. In the pursuit of God we have knelt, prostrated ourselves, and stood. We have segregated, baptized, and circumcised. We have fasted and feasted. We have blown horns, rung bells, and called to prayer. Those rituals are but colorful and diverse cultural expressions of our need for God. They are not God. Religious rituals and rules do not define morality. Rituals define community. Morality is universal, even intuitive, and wholly known in its absolute purest form by God. Every age and culture pursues that morality to the best of its ability.

Why then can a child born of the union of two religions not choose to be both? In recognizing that in being both he is honoring his father and mother; bringing two communities closer together, not preferring one community over the other. Truth is one, morality is one, God is one. How one approaches God may differ, but one approach need not negate the other in order to have a valid and true path. Is it an easy choice? No. For the currents of society are stacked against you, especially when it comes to the pragmatics of life compounded and complicated by political and social conflicts. Interfaith marriages are for the brave of heart because they do not exist in a vacuum. Couples will have their commitment and choices questioned and challenged. Religious communities tend to be less than generous: all or nothing. They define the boundaries and put up walls and security gates around access to their God. God becomes about special religious identity privileges, not about celebrating the beauty of God. If a couple can survive all of that in addition to the other natural tensions and challenges that come with most marriages, then it is certain that for better or for worse, their children will make a better world.

Leia, in answer to your question "Can I marry a Jew?" I ask you what type of Jew? One who would love and celebrate all that is Muslim in you? One who will not tire of waking up to your dimpled smile? One who will not take advantage of your ease with compromise or his ability to make you laugh even when you are very, very mad? One who in your absence will enter your bedroom to get a whiff of your lingering perfume? One who will hold you tighter and love you more when you are at your neediest and most insecure? One who will be gentle when life is tough and a little tough when you are being too gentle for life? One who will love you as I do? Leia, I would rather you marry a Jew who upholds those values than a Muslim who is a polygamist or misogynist or who does not honor your absolute equality in the eyes of God.

SEVENTEEN

Burqas and Pornography

Two Sides of the Same Coin

God intends for you ease, and He does not want to make things difficult for you.

—Quran 2:18

LEIA, HERE ARE A FEW CONFESSIONS. IF YOU were to marry a non-American Muslim, I would take comfort in knowing that because you are an American, our laws protect your marital rights. Here is why. I recently heard of a distant cousin who is not an American and who had married a Saudi. After nearly two decades of marriage, her husband decided to pursue the available but rarely executed Muslim right to take on a second wife without divorcing his first wife or giving her the choice.

Progressive, educated, and empowered, his first wife could not tolerate this demeaning arrangement. She demanded a divorce and the right to live with her children. She was denied both. Not only was she denied but she became his prisoner, for without her husband's consent she could not leave the country. An incensed and powerful family friend helped smuggle her out. For over a decade, she lived in Switzerland, where she was granted asylum and became a naturalized Swiss citizen, but was unable to so much as see her children. Finally, Interpol was able to track down the father while he was on holiday in Europe with her now estranged children and new wife and demanded that her maternal rights as a Swiss citizen be enforced.

Muslims, many of whom are insecure and defensive about Islam, will sound like apologists as they protest that this is but a rare and dramatic case. Polygamy, many of these Muslims argue, was originally intended to protect women. Under the harsh conditions of seventh-century Arabia, these marriages might have rescued widows or divorcées from squalor, or they might have provided the political and communal alliances for a vulnerable, burgeoning early Muslim community. They also point out that the Prophet remained monogamously married to his first wife, Khadijah, for twenty-five years, until her death. When he became polygamous, it was, scholars surmise, in order to break some of the social taboos and prejudices through the power of his example. He married a Christian and a Jewish woman, in addition to a divorcée.

While this interpretation in its seventh-century historical context is convincing as a progressive statement of intent, polygamy today is no longer justifiable or needed. Or as Saudi journalist Nadine al-Bedair audaciously points out in an article entitled "My Four Husbands and I": if men and women are truly equal as the Quran states they are, then women should also have the right to multiple husbands, or polyandry. She daringly and playfully makes her point:

> Allow me to choose four, five or even nine men, just as my wildest imagination shall choose. I'll pick them with different shapes and sizes, one of them will be dark and the other will be blonde. . . . They will be chosen from different backgrounds, religions, races and nations.[1]

Predictably, she unleashed the wrath of conservative clerics, who accused her of blasphemy and sued her for being anti-Muslim, for attacking Muslim traditions, and for being inflammatory and sexually provocative. More interestingly, she also reignited a debate about women's status and rights in the Muslim world. A much-needed debate, which brought out progressive clerics who endorsed the idea that polygamy has no place in the twenty-first century. One such progressive voice, Sheikh Amr Zaki, believes that it should be banned, for "in our world today, polygamy should be unacceptable. There is no need for it and, besides, no man can truly love more than one woman and vice versa."[2]

As a Muslim woman, Leia, you will run the gamut of dispa-
rate and disparaging images. Some will eroticize and others will
try to erase you. You may wonder whether Muslim women are
the seductive bathing harem harlots, historically romanticized
by Western Orientalists, or the asexual black-tented and faceless
shadows of modern radical Islam. Misogyny is brutal and dangerous when it is socially sanctioned and legally enforced. It can
make the most empowered of women feel self-conscious, belittled, and objectified. I remember how on my only visit to Saudi
Arabia as a young, fresh-faced college graduate, armed with the
ideals of my education, the pragmatics of being a woman quickly
stripped me of my academic illusions and shrank me down to my
proper size. My borrowed *abaya* felt awkward as I tripped over
its dragging hem, my stride slowed down by its billowy form and
by my discomfort with the constraint of the unfamiliar headscarf
choking me around the neck. Try as I did, my headscarf would not
stay in place; it was rejecting me as I was rejecting it. A tenacious
wisp of hair was determined to misbehave and broke free of the
veil for fresh air. The doorman stared me down as I walked into
the hotel and admonished me, gesticulating his disapproval. I re-
coiled. I was no longer first and foremost a hotel guest, a visitor, a
college graduate, a person. My womanhood overrode everything,
all other identities and roles, and it gave men, every man, including the doorman, the moral and legal authority to tell me what to
do and how to behave. My womanhood was dangerous, sexually
potent, and corrupting to men. A soft-spoken Saudi girl put it in

more poetic terms: "It is because girls are like pearls. They need to be protected." She explained, "Their beauty will tempt." I wonder if that girl would be surprised to learn that her reasoning is not particularly Muslim. It sits well with other communities who may share the same hypersexualized view of women and men's frail self-control. Views echoed in Brooklyn, where self-appointed "modesty committees" monitor the dress code of Orthodox Jewish communities. Social and economic pressure and intimidation are used to enforce compliance with dress codes that will not tempt or corrupt men. If the daughters of shop owners do not comply, then their fathers' businesses risk being shunned economically and socially. The uniforms may vary, but the intent is one. Whether it is long coats and thick stockings or black *abayas* and headscarves, the end goal is to contain and control, to establish clear female and male roles by policing morality. In Saudi Arabia, they actually have a morality police, known as *mutawa*, vigilantes whose job it is to monitor and enforce their idea of morality. Misogyny does not have one religion, but many.

Leia, you will also learn that not all veils are created equal or are cut from the same cloth. It is important to remember that, when you think of the Muslim veil, you should ask yourself which veil. There are those that are legally imposed and enforced as a matter of national or religious tyranny, but there are also those that are taken up voluntarily and readily by women. The nuances and meanings of a veil vary from one context to another. Some veils liberate and empower. In conservative societies, donning a headscarf allows women access to public places from which they would otherwise be banned. A headscarf appeases and comforts families concerned about the honor and chastity of their daughters, enabling women access to mosques, colleges, and jobs. These women wear them as armors and shields. Veils give them immunity from those who want to keep them at home. They defang small-town gossip and allow women to control their public image and affirm their moral integrity as they challenge men in traditional societies. This is how women were able to reinterpret and challenge misogynist readings of the Quran, becoming Muslim feminists. Some veils are nothing more than an individual choice. A result of a personal journey of life and faith, and maybe a desire for a closer communion with God, stripped of earthly vanities and defined by modesty of comportment and dress. Or even a statement of intent, of reform or a new desired discipline in life. A repentance for past sins, of a path lost. Akin to a nun's habit, an external expression of an internal quest for modesty, simplicity, and humility. A fine-tuning of the internal and the external. I imagine that unlike my skirmish with my imposed headscarf, when the head covering is your personal choice, there must be something comforting about the ritual of securing it as you prepare to greet the challenges of the outside world. The demarcation between the sanctuary of the inner private world and the outside public world. This is closest in spirit to a nun's habit and what it may symbolize in relation to God. Finally, there is the political veil. A veil invested in political and cultural identity. A veil taken up in defiance of all things Western, a rejection of assimilation, or a backlash. Statistics have shown an increased number of women taking up the veil in the aftermath of 9/11. This may be a reaction to the stereotypes and a feeling of otherness that many Muslims in the West have felt. The veil affirms a sense of pride and dignity in heritage. While in the fifties women marched in many Muslim countries to discard veils, today their granddaughters are fighting for the right to put them on. The right to choose and to express one's political or cultural identity is part of the many fabrics of a veil.

Leia, I imagine that as an American, your understanding of freedom, with its libertarian and individualistic undertones, will not allow you to condone a ban on the *niqab* (full face covering) even if you find it objectionable and problematic. You will find the French ban on the *niqab* too intrusive to qualify as American. But I know how offended you are by them. I remember two-year-old Taymor's reaction when he first saw them at the airport. He called them "scary ladies." I stare as I watch women in restaurants in Dubai lift their face veils in an effort to eat a meal. I cannot help it: part of me feels sad, but I also feel repulsed. I cannot even begin to imagine living publicly as an anonymous black form. Buried alive under a black tent. Invisible women. Their identities erased. No public face, denied a smile and a twinkle of the eyes. I think of my pediatrician's checklist for healthy developing babies. They track with their eyes; they lock their gazes on faces and smile. The connection is powerful, the essence of being human. A natural affirmation of one's existence; the realization and actualization of self. Denied vision, the blind touch the contours of the face. Recently, Sheikh Tantawi of Alazhar banned the *niqab* in all-girls schools. He even called it un-Islamic. He used Quranic scriptures to support his position and explained that the issue is cultural and not religious.[3] In Islam's holiest of cities, Mecca, where the annual pilgrimage is performed, face coverings are banned. Nowhere in the Quran is the face covering mentioned or prescribed. The only verse that refers to women's dress calls on them to take their *qumar*, a traditional scarf, and to cover their bosoms. Not hair or faces.

My sister protests. "Why do you take such offense?" she asks. Many women wear headscarves because it is elitist. They are saying that they are too special or regal to be seen by commoners such as you. They argue that it empowers them and liberates them from the cultural objectification of women. I say it is the objectification of women under the guise of liberation. One very long January my sister was passing time, looking for distractions while waiting for the arrival of her second born, a daughter. She set me up on Facebook; "We will be able to share pictures and keep up," she insisted when I expressed reluctance at the thought of one more technological intrusion into my life. What I did not expect was how friends whom I had lost touch with for over twenty years would find me. The first Facebook email alert read, "Are you the same Ranya Tabari of the LSE?" It was Petra Steinen, who had become a Dutch diplomat. She confirmed a date for an upcoming visit to the States and we were soon catching up over tea and biscuits

in my home. Petra expressed frustration at the resistant stereotypes and public mood in Europe concerning all things Muslim.
Some friends in Holland have asked her if she regretted naming
her daughter Soraya, a Muslim name. As she had lived in Syria
and Egypt, I wanted to know her feelings about extreme forms of
veiling. "Veiling and pornography are different sides of the same
coin," she explained, "since both are about the extreme objectification of the female form."

Leia, you will have to make up your own mind. You will have
to make peace with those who will try to brazenly impose on your
Muslim identity a Muslim uniform. To measure your faith in the
yards of fabric for a veil. Where the ideal and most pious of Muslim women are defined by their invisibility. More fabric is more
faith. They may rattle your confidence and try to make you feel
insecure. To appropriate Islam and deny your Muslim right to be
diverse. They did mine. When they do, I hope you will do as I did.
You will not allow them to dictate your truth. You will learn and
discover your own Muslim truths.

EIGHTEEN

Islam, Not "Hislam"

On Muslim Feminists

Women are the twin halves of men.

God enjoins you to treat women well, for they are your mothers,
daughters, and aunts.

The rights of women are sacred. See that women are maintained in
the rights assigned to them.

—The Prophet Muhammad

LEIA, AS YOU MATURE AS A WOMAN, YOU
will learn a lesson that all women eventually learn. Misogyny is
not limited to Muslims, nor is religion its only source. It may hark
back to a primordial memory of men's brute physical strength,
their ability to dominate and intimidate, compounded by their

sense of vulnerability when it comes to securing the paternity of their offspring. In some parts of the world, misogyny has made killing a "wayward" girl a matter of honor for the men in her family. Misogyny is resilient and is alive and well even in today's America. Who can forget Rush Limbaugh calling Sandra Fluke, a Georgetown University Law School student, a "slut" and a "prostitute" for her support for access to birth control pills?[1] From chastity belts to virginity tests and witch hunts, the push and pull of women's rights and the quest for social justice have been long and arduous.

Temples, churches, synagogues, and mosques have long been fertile grounds for misogyny and, in some cases, continue to be. Women in the Roman Catholic Church have no shortage of issues to iron out. A group that represents 80 percent of the 57,000 Catholic nuns in the United Sates, known as the Leadership Conference of Women Religious (LCWR), has been criticized by the Vatican as promoting "radical feminist themes incompatible with the Catholic faith."[2] In response to its members own experienced inequality, the Jewish Orthodox Feminist Alliance's (JOFA) mission is to expand spiritual, intellectual, and political opportunities and equality in family life, synagogues, and houses of learning within the framework of halakah or Jewish law. The commitment to work within a faith's tradition and laws in order to strive for equality and justice from within is powerful, effective, and imperative (and is so much more productive than the wholesale abandonment or condemnation of a faith). That is what Muslim feminists strive for and why they have effectively thrived. Change from within a tradition, using the references and languages of its scriptures and laws to pursue female justice and equality, is so much more convincing to those who most need it than change pursued from the outside. Western feminists, who condemn Islam as a sexist religion by definition, thereby urging women to liberate themselves from its shackles, have far less of a chance for success. Muslim women, who hold dear their faith, do not want to be told that it is bad—rather, they would like to be educated and empowered to pursue the equality and justice they believe God promises them within the framework of their culture and beliefs. In their minds, female justice, even in the most abusive of Muslim countries, will only be realized through Islam. That is the operating premise of Muslim feminists who have robustly taken on many of Islam's thorniest and most problematic issues. Armed with scripture, laws, and prophetic tradition, they disarm, nullify, negate, and hope to one day abolish the systematic abusive, misogynistic discrimination against women that is being marketed as Islam.

Leia, I hope that you will be inspired and motivated by the work of these relentless and courageous Muslim women who have chosen not to be intimidated into silence even if threatened with death. Women such as the feminist Wedad Lootah, who is a citizen of the United Arab Emirates, and who was voted one of the one hundred most powerful women in the Arab world by ArabianBusiness.com. Even though she a wears a full *niqab* (face cover) or maybe because she does, she has not shied away from

sexual topics long considered taboo by this traditionally conservative culture. Dubbed the "Dr. Ruth" of the Muslim world, she
published *Top Secret,* a sexual guidance book for married couples.
As a marriage counselor in Dubai's courthouse, she is privy to
many of the misconceptions and sexual issues that have plagued
couples in the region because of years of repression and misinfor-
mation about sexuality in Islam. Although her book was approved
by the Grand Mufti of Dubai, that has not deterred the violent
and the radical from calling her work blasphemous and issuing
death threats. What is probably not known by most is that her
work is informed by a long-standing tradition within Islam that
considers sexual pleasure a marital right for both sexes. The idea
that a Muslim woman is encouraged to fulfill her husband's sexual
needs has been used to traditionally justify many a misogynist demand on women. What is less advertised but reveals the potential
and intention for gender parity in Islam is the obligation that a
man satisfy a woman's intimate needs. A woman can even seek divorce on the grounds that a man does not sexually meet her needs.

Ghada Jamshir, a Bahraini women's rights activist, earned the
wrath of her government for speaking out against child brides,
honor killings, and polygamy. She was placed under house arrest
and lives under constant surveillance. In spite of the government's
efforts to impose a news and media blackout on her work, in 2006
Time magazine named her one of the heroes of the Arab world,
and *Forbes* magazine recognized her as one of the most effective
and powerful women of the Arab world. She believes that Muslim

family law needs to be rescued from the grip of governments who use it as a bargaining tool to placate often radical, intolerant, and extremist Islamic opposition groups. It is shamefully perverse that child brides are still justified under the veneer of Muslim prophetic tradition. That women are not safeguarded against polygamy or guaranteed the right to divorce, even though marriage in Islam is a contractual affair intended to protect the rights of a woman. Some are denied the right to their children in cases of divorce or are punitively denied a divorce altogether.

Daisy Khan, the executive director and co-founder of the American Society for Muslim Advancement (ASMA), has worked relentlessly on women's issues. Her programs include the Women's Islamic Initiative in Spirituality and Equality (WISE), which has worked globally to fulfill its mission by supporting Muslim women activists and scholars worldwide. She has launched the first Global Women's Shura (consultation) Council, with the following mission statement:

> We, members of the Global Muslim Women's Shura Council, declare gender equality to be an intrinsic part of the Islamic faith. As Muslims, we affirm our conviction that the Muslim woman is worthy of respect and dignity, that as a legal individual, spiritual being, social person, responsible agent, free citizen, and servant of God, she holds fundamentally equal rights to exercise her abilities and talents in all areas of human activity. Furthermore, we insist that these

rights are embedded within the Qur'an and six objectives of Shari'a—the protection and promotion of religion (al-din), life (al-nafs), mind (al-'aql), family (al-nasl), wealth (al-mal), and dignity (al-'ird). As the Shura Council, we embrace our collective and individual responsibility to work towards building a unified change movement of Muslim women—driven by compassion and justice—that will enable Muslim women to realize their full potential as individuals and in relationship to family, community, nation, and globe. [3]

ASMA has worked hard on projects on the ground from Egypt to Afghanistan, reeducating women using the Quran and Islamic law to increase awareness of women's rights and help eradicate practices such as female genital cutting, a cultural practice more pervasive in African countries, which continues to be justified under religious pretext.

Other Muslim feminists, such as the American Muslim scholar Amina Wadud, have led mixed congregations in prayer, officiated marriages, and advocated the viability of and necessity for women Imams.

Leia, these women are inspired by the deep-rooted conviction that the Prophet was a feminist and a maverick for his time for his belief in the equality of women and men under God. They draw their courage from a deep well of memory of often untold stories of strong women who were elemental and influential to the Prophet and early Islam. Take Khadijah, the Prophet's first wife, for example. She was Muhammad's elder, his boss, an affluent and unveiled businesswoman, and remained his only wife until her death. She audaciously proposed marriage to him and was the first Muslim, affirming Muhammad as a prophet and a messenger of God when her Christian cousin Waraqa recognized in him the prescient signs. Muslim feminists also remember the fiery, young, vivacious, and extremely bright Aisha, who was forgiven even after she set off rumors of possible infidelity when she was left behind in the desert by her caravan, only to appear the next day rescued by a young man. She accompanied Muhammad in battle, became a military leader in her own right, and earned the moniker "Mother of Islam." Effectively she became the first female lawyer, for after the death of the Prophet, the Muslim community relied on her memory and advice in matters of jurisprudence. She is credited for 2,210 Hadith (sayings attributed to the Prophet) traditions, 1,210 of which she is said to have reported directly from Muhammad. Muslim women have been given strong female role models through our storied religious tradition, and we should not let misogynist interpretations of our faith prevent us from seeking—and achieving—true equality.

NINETEEN

Apes and Swine

*We believe in God, and what was sent forth to us and what was
sent forth to Abraham and Ishmael and Isaac and Jacob, and the
tribes and whatever was given to Moses and Jesus and whatever
was given to the Prophets from their Lord; we make no distinction
between any of them.*

—Quran 2:136

*They whom God rejected and whom He condemned, and whom He
turned into apes and swine because they worshipped the powers of
evil: these are yet worse in station, and farther astray from the right
path.*

—Quran 5:59–60

"ARE YOU ONE OF THOSE MUSLIMS WHO HATES
Jews?" Leia was only twelve years old and alone, for the first time

ever, at a four-week sleepaway camp when a boy asked her what may have been a sincere question once he discovered she was not Jewish. Leia's response, "No. Are you one of those Jews who hates Muslims?" hopefully gave him something to think about. My children are growing up in New York City, which boasts the largest Jewish population in America and the second largest in the world after Tel Aviv. They have attended more temple services for friends' bar mitzvahs and bat mitzvahs than they have any services at a mosque. What that boy did not know is that my children are not only Muslims, but because I am their mother, they are also of Palestinian heritage (their father is Syrian). This can and has created interesting and dynamic coming-of-age experiences and questions. They carry within them their grandparents' and great-grandparents' memories, their stories, their loss, their pain, and their yearning. This truth, their Palestinian truth, is an inconvenient truth for many. In America, it is a story and a history that at best is little known and at worst is denied, refuted, and vilified. History has proved that it is not a truth that will die with the old and be forgotten by the young, for it has remained current and relevant even for my American children. Recently, I was surprised to receive an email invitation to a program inviting American Palestinian youth to explore their heritage through a program sponsoring and organizing visits to the Holy Land. Privately, I have often thought of Palestinians as the Jews of the twenty-first century, clearly not in terms of the Holocaust, but in many other ways. Jews and Palestinians have both been global wayfarers, banished from their land. In diaspora, they have both survived and flourished in hostile, discriminating lands, even when denied the most basic of civil rights. They have both thrived, through an industrious work ethic and an emphasis on education and strong extended family ties. The Jews were in the vanguard of culture and European civilization in spite of rampant anti-Semitism; the Palestinians have the highest literacy rates in the Arab world and are on the front line of many professions because they place such a high premium on education as a crutch for survival. The Palestinians, as the Jews before them, are begrudged and resented as a political, economic, and social threat in many of their host countries, where they are denied citizenship or equal economic and political rights. In Lebanon, at least 400,000 Palestinian refugees are restricted from some types of employment, with medicine and law being only for the Lebanese. The "Explore Your Palestinian Heritage" trips were but the latest chapter in a litany of parallel experiences, as these trips, known as "Birthright Trips" to Israel, have long been available to American Jewish youth.

The parallels I draw may already have offended. For if there is something my children have had to learn it is that Grandpa's and Grandma's memories and stories are not considered inspiring or even innocuous by many, that they actively grate at the accepted and approved "kosher" understanding of the conflict. Even though their grandparents have shared with them their stories of loss about the land that was once theirs, the homes and gardens that were not sold but abandoned in haste, and the pain and suffering that were the result of forced separations and their inability to re-turn, some will insist that this was not the case. This narrative will have you believe, and my children have experienced this firsthand, that the blame rests squarely on the Palestinians (if there is such a thing as a Palestinian—are they not "just Arabs"?), who, to quote the former Israeli prime minister Abba Eban, "never miss an op-portunity to miss an opportunity."[1]

According to this point of view, the Palestinians are at fault, and if they were more reasonable, rational, peaceful people, there would be peace. The tendency to relegate all guilt and culpability to one side may be human, but it is most certainly not effective or fair. It is also, as anyone who has ever experienced a conflict—even with a friend or spouse or offspring—can attest, the surest way of not resolving an issue. The first step in any type of conflict resolu-tion is to allow the "other side" to be heard and affirmed, even if you disagree. To acknowledge their feelings, grievances, and per-spective is half of the solution. This is not a luxury that the Pales-tinians have been allowed. Instead, my children self-edit for fear that they may offend. I remember holding my breath anxiously when Taymor told me that as part of his first-grade "share your family's stories" project he had described how his grandfather had been forced out of his home and not allowed to return. I worried that his naive six-year-old recounting of the details had inadver-tently offended his Jewish teacher. "Did you call them the bad guys?" I asked. I know that when Leia was upset by the bombing of Gaza, and a Jewish friend posted a "support Israel and blame all Palestinians for their own suffering and death" kind of post on Facebook, she quietly defriended him. "His comments upset me," she explained simply. And because my children know their grandparents, they know it is not, as Mitt Romney suggested, a question of culture that has Israel thrive and the Palestinians languish, but rather of disenfranchisement and the strangulation of occupation, censored movements, and roadblocks and punitive embargoes.[2] Instead of blaming the Palestinians for their deaths and their destruction, my children are more likely to wipe away an empathetic tear, as when, at their grandparents' home one New Year's Eve in Dubai, they caught the unavoidable footage that dominated all television coverage and I had to explain that the extravagant annual fireworks they looked forward to each year were canceled, as much of Gaza was reduced to rubble. "They are squashing them like ants," was Taymor's visual conclusion. When Leia wrote a paper for history class about the conflict, she fretted and vetted her paper for writing that might have challenged her conservative Jewish teacher's sensibilities. In spite of my fear that parents or schools may judge him as a radical, Taymor put a "Support Palestine" link on his Facebook page.

America is free, and if freedom means anything, it is the freedom to disagree, especially when the disagreement is with the majority and its conventional wisdom. We need the wisdom to understand that there are no absolute historical truths that validate and affirm: only "my narrative" and "my experiences" and "my story." So in that spirit, I have chosen to explain. I tell my children that the conflict is not just about who sits at the table and which wall and boundary and piece of land to give or keep in exchange for peace. The conflict is about two peoples who have both suffered, who come to the table with their own personal and real—not made-up or imagined—pain, suffering, and loss. A loss that my father—who at seventy-three went back to Tiberius for the first time as an American citizen to visit the home he grew up in, which still stands—knows all too well. Ironically, his family home is now a government building for the preservation of Jewish land. Weeping quietly, my father pointed out the balcony where his mother used to entertain; the mother from whom he was separated and whom he missed for a decade before learning of her unrevealed death, and whose grave he visited for closure and solace in the winter of his life. But my father was heard, and he was affirmed. For my mother described how as he stood, a few Jewish women from the neighborhood stood outside their homes and bore witness and understood his pain, for it had been their pain too, before it was his.

The way of the world is that the victor writes history, imposing or dictating the acceptable terms and desired treaties. Is that not what happened in the Spanish-American War? Is that not how Americans settled the West? And if you win land by force in war, is it not therefore yours to keep? After all, "All is fair in love and war." Or, as my Jewish friends have reminded me, they too have lost homes and art and land in Europe and the Arab world. Why do they not look to reclaim it? What makes the Palestinians so intractable? Why have they not become a footnote of history? Relegated to oblivion. The reason is that in this conflict, no real victor has emerged. Although Israel is clearly the military victor, that has proved to be far from enough. Both sides suffer in their very own and very real ways. The insidious, protracted nature of the conflict has become a way of life, compromising the health and values of both Palestinians and Israelis. Palestinians suffer because of the loss of dignity and the arduous, humiliating conditions they endure just to exist under occupation. While Gaza is nominally free, it is effectively closer to an open-air prison where trade, resources, water, ports, and airspace are controlled by Israel and its embargoes. The Israelis suffer because of the corrosive effect that decades of occupation and military service can have on the moral fabric and democratic ideals of its people and government.

The Palestinians have so far refused to become the Native Americans of the twenty-first century, living in their pockets of assigned land. This is because demographically they have not been marginalized and defanged. They remain a population that Israel cannot afford to ignore and has been unable to contain and pacify. By some estimates, they may be a majority in ten years' time. Their numbers, by the very definition of democracy, make them a demographic liability to a democratic Israel. Palestinians have proved to be more like the Jews in their deep and emotive connection to the land and their identity as a people. As such, their very existence is a challenge, representing a bifurcation of identities in a state that defines itself as Jewish, on Jewish land promised by God. Denying and negating a peoples' narrative and suffering does not a solution make. Two peoples, two stories, one land. Those are the true and real facts on the ground. The conflict can be resolved only when both sides learn to affirm each other's stories; to recognize each other's dignity, pain, and suffering in order to be able to share the land. They both need to learn that doing so does not negate their own plight: to recognize that the other's truth does not deny their truth and is not an existential threat. Dehumanizing the enemy and laying all blame at the other's doorstep does not get us closer to a solution or to justice. Humans need to be affirmed. Relationships are built on mutual respect and an affirmation of the other, even when we fundamentally disagree. That is what compromise is about, and that is how conflicts are resolved. Walls and stones, air strikes and suicide bombs, strip searches at checkpoints, and razed homes—all the while denying the suffering, humanity, and even the existence of the other—do not form the path to a resolution or a viable solution. Before there can be a solution there needs to be a fundamental affirmation of two separate and distinct narratives, and all those involved need to recognize that one narrative does not trump the other. No one side can be blamed for all the suffering, guilt, and failure. We need to learn that your truth is as important to you as your enemy's truth is to your enemy.

There are those who insist that the Palestinian-Israeli conflict is intractable and irresolvable because it is a conflict rooted in the very scripture of these two peoples: a biblical conflict of godly proportions that defies human solutions. This type of thinking is not only faulty and historically unsustainable; it is dangerous. It promotes despondency because God is conveniently blamed, relieving us of the responsibility for action. This point of view traces the conflict between Muslims and Jews all the way back to Sarah's acrimonious relationship with Hagar, who is ultimately banished from the promised land. This biblical hatred between the two peoples is reinforced by the belief that the Quran—and Muslims by extension—is by definition anti-Semitic. I am not surprised that this perception exists. Unfortunately, there are Muslims (the same Muslims who justify wife beating) who have taken a verse that does not specifically refer to Jews, but rather to those who have fatally threatened or harmed Muslims in a specific context and time in relation to a specific battle and conflict, and have removed it from its intended and limited context and used it as a horrific anti-Jewish slur. Does this negate all other Quranic verses in which the Jews are affirmed as People of the Book? The overwhelming majority of Muslims do not believe this to be true nor have they historically ever believed it. Just because there are Muslims, or Christians or Jews for that matter, who use scripture to justify their racism, does not condemn an entire religion, its history, or its faith to a condition of permanent racism. The truth of the matter is that all scriptures have within them the tendency to be racist or discriminatory, and all have been used at one time or another to that effect. That does not make all Christians or all Jews or all Muslims racist. There are enough Jews and Christians who have made racist remarks about Muslims. If some Christians blame Jews for killing Jesus, a view that has historically been used to promote anti-Semitism and hate, does that make all Christians racist and anti-Semitic? Christianity, Judaism, and Islam are not immune; nor is Buddhism, which today is being used in Nepal to persecute Muslims. This does not mean that we should condemn an entire tradition and its people. We should, on the other hand, hold the perpetrators of these views responsible, and we should assume active responsibility for hate speech and vilification by promoting heightened awareness and reeducation. It is imperative that all religions develop and promote an awareness of the unacceptability of hateful speech, especially when it is spoken as if it were God's truth. There is no room for a racist God in this century.

TWENTY

"In Any War between the Civilized Man and the Savage, Support the Civilized Man"[1]

*God is the Light of the heavens and the earth. The Parable of His
Light is as if there were a Niche and within it a Lamp: the Lamp
enclosed in glass: the glass as it were a brilliant star: Lit from a
blessed Tree, an Olive, neither of the east nor of the west, whose
oil is well-nigh luminous, though fire scarce touched it: Light upon
Light! God doth guide whom He will to His Light.*

—Quran 24:35

THE FIRST TIME I READ SAMUEL P. HUNTING-
ton's seminal 1993 *Foreign Affairs* article entitled "The Clash of
Civilizations?," which proposed that a clash between the Christian West and the Muslim East would help define many of the
world's modern conflicts, I was still single and a student. It created a personal paradox for me then and it continues to do so
now. According to Huntington, the conflict between Western
and Muslim civilizations is a deep-rooted, 1,300-year-old historical conflict that can be traced all the way back to the Crusades
and the defeat of the Moors by the Franks at the Battle of Tours
in AD 732. Religion, values, and culture are not only some of
the many factors contributing to the world's relations between
nation-states but, according to Huntington, they are the most important defining paradigms through which we can make sense of
our modern world; never mind economic, colonial, or geopolitical power struggles and the struggle for human dignity and individual freedoms and rights. Culture and religion would make for
a world comprised of the "West against the rest," a world where
"the rest" reject Western values and culture.[2] This point of view
assumes a clear demarcation between Judeo-Christian values,
which translate into values of democracy, individual rights, and
freedoms born out of European history, and Muslim values, which

by definition reject this as a foreign, Western, liberal point of view. Muslim culture and civilization, on the other hand, are identified by dictatorships, theocracies that reject democracies, censorship, oppression, and traditionalism. This point of view reinforces the idea that the Judeo-Christian West is fundamentally at odds in values and culture with the Muslim world; it has become the Holy Grail for many leaders and foreign policy experts in the West. Its populist, crowd-pleasing expression can be heard in remarks made by Western leaders such as Germany's chancellor Angela Merkel, who declared in 2010 to enthusiastic applause: "Germany is a Christian nation, inspired by a Christian understanding of human rights. We don't have too much Islam, we have too little Christianity. We have too few discussions about the Christian view of mankind."[3]

The clash of civilizations paradigm has found long legs in the West and eager Muslim bedfellows in the "rest": Muslims who reject all things Western as if they were the plague. Now that I am married and have two American-born Muslim children, this presumed clash is not just an abstract paradox, but rather feels intimately unsavory and confusing to my family. We are after all culturally Western—American, to be specific—but spiritually and religiously Muslim. Where are we as a family in this clash of civilizations? That is what I found myself wondering as I made my way to a lacrosse game, carpooling with a teammate's dad. In a conversation about American foreign policy, he casually remarked how Huntington had it right. America's conflict with the

Muslim world was nothing short of a clash of civilizations: an inevitable, preordained, historically predetermined conflict of values, religion, and culture. I chose not to disagree. I sat quietly but uncomfortably in the passenger seat, wondering if that meant that he thought my Muslim family's core values were at odds with America's values. Or whether he unconsciously and subliminally suspected that our loyalty and commitment to those American values enshrined in the Constitution—freedom of speech, worship, and belief—could be jeopardized by our Muslim values. Did he believe that as Muslims, or in order for us to be true and authentic Muslims, we would have to reject the separation of church and state, the rule of secular democratic laws, and the guarantees of freedom of speech?

I am certain that the answer is yes if he accepts a reactionary and radical Islam as the only acceptable and legitimate Islam. A fascist and xenophobic Islam that cannot be compassionate, just, and tolerant of individual freedoms and collective human rights. A reactionary, dictatorial Islam that is born out of the conflicts of colonialism and the racism of imperialism and its "white man's burden" to civilize those it deems uncivilized. An Islam used by absolute rulers as an arsenal in their political will to rule absolutely. This is a reactionary Islam that is not born out of a fundamental conflict in values, but rather one that allows modern political, social, and cultural conflicts to dictate its values. Muslim values do not create the conflict but radical Muslim values are a byproduct of the conflict. A byproduct of regimes and of Muslims who blithely use modern Western technology to arm their security forces, bomb their citizens, and spy on their conversations. Muslims who are only too happy to purchase the latest Western gadget or toy, but glorify and subscribe to the social rules and mores of a mythical and imagined Muslim insular past at war with all things Western. Especially if the rejection of all things Western allows them to repress at will, reject democracy as un-Muslim, and pander to extremists or Muslim opposition groups and those elements in society who are traumatized by the rapid forces of modernization, all the while maintaining their absolute hold on power as God's soldiers on earth. Islam is theirs to define and dictate and impose at will to the exclusion of all other Muslim opinions and plurality of thought. Islam becomes intolerant of diversity of thought and individual choice, eagerly damning those who disagree as heretics and infidels. Muslim values and laws are dictated by decree and through absolute rulers, and as we know from Lord Acton, "Absolute power corrupts absolutely."[4] If these are indeed Muslim values, then they are threatening to Muslims and non-Muslims alike.

Without choice there is no morality. And no, inshallah or "God willing," is not testimony to the fatalistic nature of Muslims who are ordained to defer all things to God, and are therefore a whole list of stereotypes that Orientalists have imagined them to be. Muslims who seek to impose by decree what they believe are Muslim values are effectively removing the individual's right to choose. Those who try to legalize Muslim morality through decrees that ban alcohol, dictate modesty, and impose acceptable

Muslim social behavior are effectively banning choice, which is the essence and the heart and mind of morality. Without choice, without the *right* to choose, we have God by decree. Values and morality imposed by decree are not morality. Prohibition is not morality. Freedom is morality. Freedom to make the right moral choice is the essence of morality. That is when it matters and when it counts. Prohibition and repression breed corruption, hypocrisy, and contempt. They breed duplicitous societies where alcohol is smuggled, grape juice is fermented in bathtubs, and hard liquor is overconsumed. Where girls undergo hymen restoration surgeries to maintain the appearance of chastity and virginity. They breed societies where what "seems" is more important than what is.

Truth has a resilience that endures and perseveres no matter its abuse. The truth is that which binds us in our common humanity, operating outside the confines of cultures, religion, and peripheral values of traditions, rituals, and manners. Peripheral values may determine how or when we pray, to whom we pray, and where we pray. Values that are expressions of the diversity of approaches to God are just that: an expression of the diversity of our human quest and expression for God. But then there are core values that operate outside the cultural and the peripheral: the sanctity of life, our equality in the eyes of God no matter our race, sex, ethnicity, or religion. Our need to give and to protect the weak, to be charitable to those who are not as privileged. To be kind and honest and just. To respect those who may differ from us. To allow for freedom of thought and individual choice without fear for one's life. These are *human* rights, not only Christian rights. They are Muslim rights and Hindu rights and Buddhist and Jewish and atheist rights. Never has this truth been as relevant as it is today. Historically, Muslim civilizations have always been adept at adopting, assimilating, and integrating preexisting values, traditions, music, science, poetry, art, and architecture. Cultural gatekeepers guarding against the infiltration of foreign and alien values and traditions are by definition insular, xenophobic, and limited. Fortunately, in the age of the Internet, social media, and global reach, they are also on the wrong side of history. To assume a clash of civilizations with stark and conflicting purity of values and demarcation lines and barriers is preposterous and unintelligent. The idea that we can categorize with purity that which is Islamic and that which is un-Islamic, Christian or un-Christian, when it comes to core values of human justice and dignity and sanctity of human life is absurd. Just as there is no purity of race, there is no purity of morality exclusive to one faith tradition but not the other. Are there differences of approach? Of course there are. Democracy may not usher in Western-style liberalism, and freedom may find its ultimate expression in conservatism and traditionalism, but what is nonnegotiable are our core values of justice, diversity, and the individual's protected freedom to choose with dignity.

I had started out with a crisis of faith. Aisha was my catalyst; her stoning death and its injustice I chose to make my personal injustice. I brought her to the center of my world, regardless of how far removed her reality was. I chose to make her crime my personal Muslim affront. I worried that I would be left isolated, spiritually stranded. Instead, I have found my faith reinforced and fortified, reenergized by progressive Muslims, thinkers, poets, artists, and journalists, academics who refuse to be disenfranchised from Islam. They have refused to be ignored, belittled, or silenced. If there is anything that has relegated the idea of the "clash of civilizations" to the cemetery of ideas, it is the Arab Spring. Although its success is far from guaranteed and its conclusion is far from secured, its impulse, its original spark, is a testimony to the power and truth of those core values that bind us as humans, regardless of our civilizations. The Arab Spring and the hundreds of thousands who are now struggling and dying are a potent expression of the need for Muslims and non-Muslims in that part of the world to live as active, dignified citizens of governments that protect and empower them, and not as lesser, repressed subjects. Their revolutions are ultimately about honor and self-respect. It is about their urgent need to be global citizens who are neither stigmatized nor shamed by their governments, leaders, or religion into being lesser individuals who belong to lesser cultures, civilizations, and faiths. They take their courage and their fortitude, their resolve and passion, from the belief that God is justice. That God's justice is greater than any human interpretation of that justice or any man-made laws that try to regulate that justice. That God is by definition on the side of justice over tyranny, corruption, and oppression. Totalitarian dictatorships are not the defining hallmarks of Muslim civilization: they were but its latest, darkest hour. Those who continue to challenge these regimes have, with their courage and lives, debunked the core tenets of those who continue to insist that the world is defined by a clash of civilizations. They are proof that although the "arc of the moral universe may be long," as Martin Luther King Jr. reminded us, "it bends toward justice." Ultimately, those core values that are absolute and common to all are more a function of education than of temperament or intellect. My children's identities will not be a paradox, but an inspiration. It is more accurate today to speak of the *complicity* of civilizations. Of the candor, collaboration, and cooperation of civilizations as we move forward together to solve, heal, cure, and advance in our quest for God's irrefutable and absolute values.

TWENTY-ONE

Proud Muslims, Not Lesser Muslims

Let There Be Joy

God is beautiful and loves beauty.

One hour in the pursuit of knowledge is better than a thousand prayers.

—The Prophet Muhammad

WHEN MY FATHER-IN-LAW HEARD THAT I WAS writing about Islam, he asked, "Why?" It may seem like a strange question to an outsider, but in many ways it is elemental to the story. We are by and large secular Muslims and yet, in spite of the stigma against Islam in the West—a stigma that we have wrestled with and one that we are called upon to explain, especially after "Muslims" commit terrorist attacks—we continue to choose to identify as Muslims. We do this for many reasons, not least of which is that we refuse to be told that we are lesser Muslims. Let me explain. My Faith Club had come out of retirement for a radio program producer named J.J. and her mother. We met J.J. when she booked us for Gayle King's show on Oprah Radio. She had learned about our book through her mother, who called her insisting that she pick up a copy of her own. J.J. had grown up in Virginia Beach, the daughter of an interfaith marriage: her mother is Jewish and her father is Christian. She describes herself as Jewish but with an acute sensitivity and appreciation for Christianity. What she never would have anticipated is how Islam would also be added to her personal religious mix. As a young woman she moved to New York, and at her local deli, she fell in love. He worked behind the counter, a Yemenite with a heavy accent, and a Muslim. *The Faith Club* spoke to her heart and her mind. Once married, they were thinking of starting a family, but J.J. had many questions and a few apprehensions about the future religious identity of her children. J.J.'s mother, who had started her own Faith Club in her community, mobilized various interfaith organizations and planned our visit to Virginia Beach. Over 200 people turned up at the local Jewish Community Center, where chairs were lined shoulder to shoulder on what normally functioned as a basketball court. J.J.'s life and her accomplishments were honored and recognized and she was celebrated as a valued daughter of the community.

At the end of the presentation, we opened up the session to
questions, and that's when a veiled young woman wearing a colorful *hijab* of vivid purple and blue jewel tones stood up. Tall and
proud, she stood erect as she addressed the audience. She began
with a clarification: lest anyone be under the impression that she
had been forced to wear her head covering, she wanted to make
it clear that it was her choice. Her tone was friendly but defensively defiant. Feeling her vulnerability, I tried to support her by
elaborating on some of the misconceptions regarding veiling in
Islam. I confirmed that many women were indeed taking up the
hijab as a feminist statement that empowered them to read and
interpret scripture. Others, I continued, adopted a headscarf out
of piety and modesty, or for cultural expression. I explained that
what was most essentially important for all to remember was that
the veil was a choice, not mandated in the Quran, and one that
does not necessarily define all Muslim women. I was oblivious
to the reaction my response must have triggered, but she did not
waste any time. As I was stepping outside into the crisp spring air,
she approached me, fortified by a group of friends. "The veil is
not cultural; it is Muslim and it is required by Islam," she insisted.
"And how can you say that if you don't pray five times a day, that
you are still a Muslim? The pillars are like the foundations of the
house of Islam: remove one and then the house is not sound." In
spite of her unapologetic skepticism, I tried to explain: "I take no
issue with your choices and your beliefs: they are yours. I just don't
feel that ritualistic prayer is fundamental to my relationship with

God. I pray but in my own time and place." "Well then, you are not a Muslim" was her damning conclusion. By her judgment, 80 to 85 percent of Muslims do not qualify as Muslims either. According to Oxford professor Tariq Ramadan, "Only 15 to 20 percent of Muslims around the world actively follow their religion's precepts—that is to say, pray five times a day, attend Friday early-afternoon prayers (the most significant prayer session of the week for Muslims), abstain from alcohol, and follow the other commandments and prohibitions of traditional Islam."[1] Secular Muslims may comprise the majority of the population in some Muslim countries.

I am a Muslim for many reasons. I am a Muslim to remind those who prefer to wear their religion literally on their heads that theirs is but one of many choices: not the only choice and not the only gateway to God. I remain a Muslim so that those who feel self-righteous in their piety and arrogant in their certainty may be reminded to be humble again. Maybe, one day, we will come to realize that God might not be as preoccupied with what you choose to put or not put on your head, but with what you do with your life—that a Muslim's identity may be better judged by service, charity, and love for all rather than an obsession with the female form.

I am a Muslim to remind Muslims that religiosity and piety are not morality. Religion and rituals are but cultural expressions of our desire to know God, to commune with God. They are but symptoms of our efforts. Rules and rituals are not values in and of themselves. They are a means of bringing God into our lives. Justice and ethics are not arrived at through piety alone. It is a sad state of affairs when we need to remind ourselves that a devout and pious Muslim is not a radical or violent Muslim, but it is also important to remember that piety does not necessarily equate with morality. Normative values are arrived at by thinking and questioning, not by emulating blindly. According to Dr. Khaled Abou El Fadl, a professor of Islamic law at UCLA, Muslim civilization has both most honored and most betrayed its book.[2] He reminds us how the Prophet told his followers, "An hour's reflection is better than a year's worship."[3] And when his followers, puzzled, asked him if it is "even better than reading the Qu'ran," he answered, "And, can the Qur'an be useful without knowledge?" In the Quran, Muslims are reminded not to accept any information unless they verify it for themselves: "I have given you the hearing, the eyesight, and the brains, and you are responsible for using them."[4] For those who continue to cherry-pick verses to affirm their ideas and inclinations, they are reminded in the Quran that "He (God) has sent down to you (Muhammad) this book which contains some verses that are categorical and absolute and others that are equivocal. But those who are twisted of mind look for equivocal verses seeking deviations and giving them interpretations of their own but none knows their meaning except God."[5] The most important values, those that are the foundation of any godly life, are universal values that cannot be confined or limited to one tradition. Values are most valuable and effective when they make justice their ultimate goal. Different faith traditions may have different approaches to those values, but no tradition has a monopoly on justice.

I am a Muslim to remind Muslims that the tension between orthodoxy and progressives is not exclusively Muslim. Orthodox Jewish women may have more in common with orthodox Muslim women than they do with their own coreligionists. Religious tensions and differences in interpretation are inherent in all faith traditions. Muslim secularists are not necessarily rejecting their faith. Many do not want to be at the mercy of orthodox Muslims who have appointed themselves as guardians of the faith and who define faith strictly through observance of rituals. Many secularists do not want to be denied the possibility of spiritually rich lives. They are often inspired by Muslim values and the belief in the transcendent, beyond the here and now of life. Many secular Muslims are not happy just committing to humanistic or secular ideals, but insist on their right to be inspired by Islam's rich plurality of traditions and culture. They do not believe that orthodoxy has sole proprietorship over God and the good Muslim life. The schism between secularists who choose to believe and those who are orthodox is exaggerated and inflamed to empower orthodoxy to define the boundaries of faith. America's gift is that it has protected the rights of all by separating church and state and safeguarding the freedom of worship for all Americans in their glorious diversities. The most important prayer in Islam asks God to guide Muslims to the path of righteousness, "the path of whom you have blessed, not those who have been led astray."[6] The righteous path is, first and foremost, defined by justice and mercy: justice and mercy for those who are weak, vulnerable, different, or unprotected. These values are more meaningful when they are applied to those who do not look, worship, or think like us. They are most needed when we are most challenged, and by those who have sinned most. Before every prayer, Muslims are required to address God as "the most merciful and compassionate," or "*Al Rahman, Al Raheem.*" Traditionally, you cannot pray or read the Quran before uttering this most frequently whispered invocation: "In the name of God, the most merciful and compassionate God." Righteousness is not emulating the life of the Prophet as he lived in seventh-century Arabia, but placing his life and practices in their proper context and recognizing the moral lessons and guidelines they were meant to exemplify. Judged in the context of his time, the Prophet of Islam was a maverick, a feminist, and a thinker. He exemplified morality for his time: we need to follow his example and live morally in our time.

I am a Muslim because I refuse to be at the mercy of Salafists and Wahhabis who have usurped Islam as an identity, dictating and controlling what it means to be a Muslim. They have left Muslims spiritually compromised and vulnerable. Their understanding of what it means to be a Muslim is not ahistorical but anti-historical.[7] Their insidious ideas—arrived at by aping imagined or idealized Muslim social, behavioral, and legal norms limited to seventh-century Arabia—actively and willingly ignore at least ten centuries of evolving and diverse Muslim thought and Muslim civilizations that spanned vast geographical regions stretching from Spain to Turkey, Damascus, Jerusalem, Iraq, Samarkand, India, and Africa. Wahhabi and Salafist preoccupation with reliving the seventh century has produced bizarre modern edicts in the name of Islam: banning women from driving or traveling at will, enabling men to marry fourteen-year-old girls, and maiming and stoning in the name of Muslim honor and justice. My Islam is the Islam of the "1001 Inventions: The Enduring Legacy of Muslim Civilization" exhibit. This touring exhibit first opened at the Science Museum in London and commemorates and celebrates the many Muslims who have been at the forefront of seeking knowledge from the cradle to the grave: the Islam of astrology, cartography, alchemy, physics, geometry, philosophy, and poetry.

I am a Muslim to remind Muslims that diversity is indeed the sign of divine mercy. I am a Muslim because Islam, with all its heart, soul, and mind, is at its genesis an ecumenical faith that has always believed that for every nation, God has sent its messenger. Muslim monotheism is so absolute that it qualifies both God and all his attributes as One: including his creation, our universe, and its people. The diversity of theologies, rituals, and approaches to God does not deny or negate the Oneness of God. We as humans in all our glorious differences and diversities are linked and share God's one absolute universal truth. At the end of the day the God we choose to glorify can have many qualities, often contradictory and all within the same scriptures. What our God looks like, what we think he is looking for, and what values we attribute to God are often a reflection of who we are as humans; where we are culturally as a civilization. Religion is not a belief system that exists in a vacuum. Individuals, societies, and governments leave their impressions on religions. An angry, insecure person will most likely have an angry, insecure God. A gracious, forgiving individual will often have a forgiving God. We color God with our humanity and therefore put religion at risk. I have often felt that we need to rescue God from the abuse he has suffered at the hands of our humanity: individuals, states, and organizations. I am a Muslim to remember that Islam can be a religion that is more about what you can do than what you cannot do.

I am a Muslim because I do not want to leave my children spiritually stranded and vulnerable to what others tell them Islam can or cannot be. Minorities are often defined by the feature that differentiates them from the majority. How the majority judges or perceives that distinguishing feature is crucial to the formation of identity. Because horrific acts of terror continue to be committed in the name of Islam—most recently, the Boston Marathon bombings and the barbaric, gruesome beheading of a young soldier in Great Britain—Islam elicits passionate opinions and feelings, at a minimum intense curiosity or scrutiny or fear. Islam is a lightning rod of emotions, all of them passionate and intense. For this reason, my children cannot be detached, neutral, or indifferent to that component of their identity. Either they will reject and distance themselves from Islam, liberating themselves from the questions and curiosities, or, if they continue to call themselves Muslims, they will need to have clarity of thought in the fog of fear, confusion, and hate. If I do not help them find the answers to the challenges and questions they will surely face as Muslims, then I will leave them vulnerable to reactionary, radical, and violent positions from Muslims and non-Muslims. By nurturing and educating their Muslim identity, I know that they will not believe for a minute that to be a devout Muslim is to reject celebrating American holidays such as Thanksgiving or Martin Luther King's birthday. Or that Islam is about violent vigilantism that avenges perceived injustices through murder. When progressive or secular Muslims do not self-identify as Muslims or are made to feel that they are lesser Muslims or not-quite Muslim, they surrender the religion to extremists, to those who are less than tolerant, or to Islamophobes. Should my children ever feel the need for spiritual solace or for a more ritualistic commitment to Islam, I trust that they will not be at the mercy of radical interpretations or the sick logic of the violent. By defining what being Muslim is for my family I help mold and enlighten their Muslim identities, empowering them as Muslims with an educated voice and an enlightened point of view. They will not be cowed by either Muslims or non-Muslims who challenge and abuse their faith.

I am a Muslim to remind Muslims of the Muslim adage that God is beautiful and loves beauty. If justice is the mind of Islam, then union with the beauty of God is its heart. Muslims need to remember that there is an Islam other than the joyless, angry Islam that has metastasized as the recognized Islam. I want to re-mind Muslims that God is not a punitive God of fear, concerned with what you cannot do, but rather a forgiving God, inspiring what you can do. I am a Muslim to remind Muslims that you can be a Muslim and fly a kite. *Basant,* a colorful Pakistani rite of spring celebration, which involved much merrymaking and kite flying, was banned five years ago, ostensibly to protect the public from the hazards of kite flying, which had resulted in a number of accidents. The truth is more sinister. Jamaat ud Dawa, a mili-tant Pakistani Islamicist group, warned against holding the ritual because it deemed it un-Islamic and contradictory to Pakistan's Muslim identity, which it has aggressively cultivated as its rai-son d'être since becoming a state. As a result, the economy has suffered in the region. Punjabi women can no longer use their sewing skills to create the colorful intricate kites that were flown in celebration of spring. An entire industry has been decimated; tourism and its welcome and much-needed profits have also been obliterated. There is an obsession with the purity of the Muslim identity, one based on a singular limited and blighted definition of culture and history that denies centuries of historical and cultural alchemies and political realities. Any obsession with purity of race, identity, ethnicity, or Muslim culture is egregious and grievous and nothing short of a benighted symptom of an arrested culture, faith, and people. For the sake of us all, let there be joy!

TWENTY-TWO

Proud Americans,
Not Lesser Americans

America, a Love Story

Oh mankind! We created you from a single (pair) of a male and a female, and made you into nations and tribes, that you may know each other (not that you may despise each other).

—Quran 49:13

LAST SUMMER MY FATHER, LOVE, AND GOD were on my mind. A decade ago, my father was diagnosed with an aortic aneurism. The aorta, the main artery to the heart, was gradually thinning out at three separate points. As long as measurements of the aortic wall were below a certain number, all he had to do was maintain a healthy lifestyle and monitor his condition annually. The dreaded numbers were finally delivered. Any more distention, his doctors explained, would put him at risk of instant death since the pressure of his pulsating blood could collapse the aortic walls. He was seventy-eight years old and a diabetic, so his surgery was higher risk than high risk. It was scheduled for the third of October, my birthday month. Face to face with his mortality, I felt the urgency of life. Those big questions that used to keep me up when life was still an imagined adventure I was waiting to embark on, full of "ifs" and "firsts," came back to haunt me.

I am anchored now by a life more than half lived, defined by concrete experiences, realities, and responsibilities; more tempered in my expectations. I recognize the God I have submitted to at challenging moments in my life in my father's serene courage and quiet acceptance. In the way he shares his onion soup with me (even though soup is really not meant to be shared), and in the way he looks at me at lunch. He is of a generation of men who do not speak love: they act love. They do not voice their feelings, and yet somehow you understand. Once, my younger self asked him why he had never told us he loved us. By contrast, parents today drop an "I love you" as a "good night" in every camp letter or farewell. "The more you love," he tried to explain, "the harder it is to say." At the time, I judged him naively: *It makes no sense,* I thought. Today I understand. Love as a word has become a little trite. As a lyric in love songs or the promise of fidelity in a flourishing romance it may suffice, but then there is an ineffable love. A love so sacred that it can feel confined and compromised by mortal words. I have been told that the Jewish God is protected in a similar way.

With the date of the surgery looming ever nearer, every rising sun rendered a poetic sadness to even the happiest of moments (lunch with his grandchildren, parcels of unexpected gifts given for no reason, small splurges for his birthday); his reticence was betrayed. Wax lyrical he did not, but I hung on to those elusive words, addressed not to me but to his wife, my mother, by way of confession: "I love my children, Aida." I saw God in his reflective, serene courage, unheroic and unceremonious but quiet and resolute. I saw a willful, omnipotent God in his clenched determined jaw, betrayed by its errant quivering; in that final moment he was finally rolled away from us, alone, as we all will be one day, as we face our one certain common destiny. So God has been much on my mind.

God was also on the mind of the Democrats and the Republicans in the summer of 2012 as they prepared for the upcoming presidential elections. At the Republican National Convention, God was mentioned twelve times in the official platform.[1] God was then added to the Democratic National Convention platform by special presidential request. Atheists complained that God should not be in political platforms, and secularist decrees on the death of God in the political and public sphere have proved to be wrong. God is politically omnipresent, current and relevant. Our elections have morphed into culture wars on values in America: from abortion, to gay marriage, to birth control pills and sex education. This modern God is very much in our lives, in our bedrooms, in our schools, informing our medical research, our offices, and even our food. God is called on to redeem and forgive politicians who have strayed, to win elections, and most importantly to define what it means to be American today. God has even been invoked to target religious minorities and desecrate holy books to purge the un-American out of America. Social media, blogging, and tweeting have given new meaning to the truism that all politics is local. Local now is anywhere from Karachi to Kansas. Our global intimacy can and has had serious consequences, where the clamorous few—those who choose to agitate and incite and terrorize—gain instant infamy, giving them a disproportionate degree of power and impact on our lives. The ensuing firestorms have proved deadly in countries experiencing social, political, and revolutionary tumult, as well as, heartbreakingly, in our own backyards. This environment is why it is vital that we talk about God, rather than pretend that God does not exist in the public sphere, vital that we reflect and try to understand. "In God We Trust" is on our dollar bills, a congressionally approved national motto and a testimony to America's deep spiritual roots. It is our acknowledgment that there is a transcendent, bigger, and more powerful entity than us as a nation. That we as a nation aspire to those esteemed and divine values of love, respect, and justice for all.

The real world brings real challenges and cruel limitations to those ideals. American Muslims know that many Americans do not feel that theirs is a God they can trust. Every time there is a violent attack, from Newtown, Connecticut, to the Boston Marathon bombings, American Muslims live in the purgatory of their identity, which does not allow them to mourn and grieve without the added anxiety of having to worry about the religious or ethnic identity of the perpetrator. "Please let it not be a Muslim," we plead as we struggle with the shame and complications of our inevitable culpability by association, of reinforced stereotypes as suspect Americans. It is for this reason that mocking and deriding President Obama as a secret Muslim works well for his political detractors. "Muslim" is a slur, used effectively to undermine our president and categorize him as "other" than American. But American Muslims do indeed place their trust in America's God. Because we are passionately in love with the "Big Idea" that is America: an idea that is nothing short of Divine. America's nascent ideals have proved to be more powerful and resilient than the contradictions of its reality and historical struggles. Contradictions in the slave-owning Thomas Jefferson, a stalwart of American liberty, freedom, and equality. Contradictions in our historical propensity to go on witch hunts, from outcast women in Salem, Massachusetts, to Communists in Washington, DC, or in our periodic "nativist" fears, which have made us qualify and limit the immigration of certain groups. America's ideals, enshrined and revered and protected in our Constitution, endure and empower and heal. They gave birth to Martin Luther King Jr. and Rosa Parks. When lynch mobs and Jim Crow laws banned blacks from places ranging from bars to boardrooms, the tenacity and audacity of America's promise triumphed time and time again. That is why a little boy from Hawaii with a funny name like Barack Hussein Obama could not only dream to be—but *be*—our president.

With every victory America is more robust in its convictions, empowering a new generation of immigrants: Chinese, Japanese, and Jewish. With the affirmation of each new generation of American diversity, the infallibility of the American dream is preserved and its moral authority perseveres. Its legacy is a beacon to the world and to its own newly minted Americans. When American Muslims salute the flag and take the oath, they are bowing at the altar of America's one and most important religion, which preempts all other differences and diversities: it is an American faith in the elixir of its ideals. Although historically those ideals have been tested, corrupted, and appropriated to the exclusion of others, time and time again it is not cynicism that sets in but a resilient faith that a better America will reign supreme. Few other country's narratives, national myths, and stories have that level of rapture. And those that do are usually founded on the idea that only a certain ethnicity, religion, or color need apply. America's miracle—its vitality—is its ability to deliver its promise from one century to the next to different groups of people. Which other country has asked, "Give me your tired, your poor, / Your huddled masses yearning to breathe free, / The wretched refuse of your teeming shore. / Send these, the homeless, tempest-tost to me, / I lift my lamp beside the golden door!"?

America's secularism is a fervent religious belief that the best
way to protect God from man, and man from man, is to separate church and state. The God America trusts has historically
not been confined to or defined by one faith. Even the most ardent Islamophobes do not seek to negate or circumvent America's
ideals but aim to protect those ideals from what they believe to be
the enemy: Islam. Islam is the un-American villain precisely because Islamophobes believe that it threatens and sabotages those
cherished ideals. Islam is believed to be by definition anti-West-
ern, anti-American, and anti-freedom: immutably violent, regressive, archaic, and oppressive. Islamophobes claim not to have
anything against Muslims—just Islam, from which they hope to
rescue Muslims. They do not recognize another type of Islam. Of
course, there is no such thing as one Islam. There is a Saudi Islam
and an Egyptian Islam, all defined and molded by their respec-
tive cultures and political and social environments. A religion is
only as enlightened or peaceful or plural or tolerant as the hands
in which it finds itself. It is such a simple idea, but one that is
obstinately overlooked. There are as many types and nationalities
of Muslims as there are Muslim experiences. American Muslims
recognize Islam's ideals—God's ideals—in the very idea of America. They see the synergy between Muslim values they have loved
and continue to love and America's values, which have allowed a
plurality and diversity of faith traditions to thrive and feel secure.
In America, they can truly trust "in God": a God who is protected
from the state, from the vanities and greed of man. For God, in far

too many majority Muslim countries, is a God in service of man, vulnerable to the tumult and abuse of societies and states that have not yet safeguarded and protected those ideals.

Recently, I was asked what it means for us to be Muslims. The casual observer sees a predominantly secular home where spirituality and prayer are practiced individualistically and in our own time and on our own terms. I may not kneel in formal ritualistic prayers five times a day with the prerequisite ablutions, but there is not a day when I do not pray, grateful for our many blessings: for my father, who miraculously pulled through eleven hours of surgery, for Dr. Daniel Clair, to whose hands God entrusted the saving of so many lives. For the countless human mercies, love, and beauty I whisper, "There is no god but God; and Muhammad is his Prophet."

Why have I then made Islam an important component of my children's identity, when it might have been easier to do otherwise? Why do we as a family refuse to leave it behind, condemn it or distance ourselves from it? The ramifications of 9/11 and the ensuing stereotypes reinforced by headline news and active war zones in Muslim countries have created a fear of Islam and confusion about what it is to be Muslim. For many, either you are guilty of being a Muslim or you are not really a Muslim. Either you are a "bad" Muslim or you are a "good" secular non-Muslim. An exception. Our journey has been about refusing to be denied our simultaneous Muslim and American identities. By no uncertain measure, we choose to be Muslims because we refuse to be lesser Americans. We are Muslims not only because of our religious credo but also because of our faith in America's credo. For if we do not insist on being Muslims who are equal to Christians, Jews, Buddhists, and Mormons, we are ultimately lesser Americans; and America is less American. We insist on being Muslims for faith and God, and for country. We refuse to be lesser Americans who belong to a lesser America, an America that has forgotten its promise. Every time America has successfully ironed out the contradictions in its promise, it has emerged more robust and confident. America may be challenged in the future by other rising global economic or military powers. However, there is not one power or country that can challenge the idea of America. Its heart and soul are in its historic promise, its superpower ability to welcome, assimilate, and empower those who continue to flock to its shores. That is truly America's unrivaled, unmatched power, pride, and legacy. It is our own.

NOTES

PROLOGUE

1. "Anti-Muslim Sentiments Fairly Commonplace," Gallup, July 28, 2006, accessed June 28, 2013, http://www.gallup.com/poll/24073/antimuslim -sentiments-fairly-commonplace.aspx.
2. "TIME Poll Results: Americans' Views on the Campaign, Religion and the Mosque Controversy," *Time*, August 18, 2010, http://content.time.com /time/politics/article/0,8599,2011680,00.html.
3. Ibid.
4. Rachel L. Swarns, "Halliburton Subsidiary Gets Contract to Add Temporary Immigration Detention Centers," *New York Times*, February 4, 2006, accessed February 2, 2012, www.nytimes.com/2006/02/04/national/04halliburton.html ?_=2&oref=login.

CHAPTER 1

1. Hadith: Muslim oral tradition of the Prophet's sayings.
2. Abdullah Yusuf Ali, *The Glorious Qur'an Translation*, reprint (New Delhi: Islamic Book Service, 2006), 17:23–24.

    Note to reader: I have relied primarily on three English translations of the Quran, and have taken the liberty to choose those that I feel are most expressive of its original Arabic and spiritual meaning. All further citations of the Quran are either from this translation or from *The Sublime Quran*, trans. Laleh Bakhtiar, 6th ed. (Chicago: Kazi Publications, 2009), or *The Quran*, trans. T. B. Irving, 1999, reprint (New Delhi: Goodword Books, 2003).
3. Cyril Glasse, *The Concise Encyclopedia of Islam*, rev. ed. (London: Stacey International, 2001), 470.

CHAPTER 2

1. Richard Ferber, *Solve Your Child's Sleep Problems*, rev. ed. (New York: Touchstone, 2006).

CHAPTER 3

1. Cyril Glasse, *The Concise Encyclopedia of Islam*, rev. ed. (London: Stacey International, 2001), 470.
2. Quran 5:44.
3. Quran 17:1 and Hadith (Muslim oral traditions of the Prophet's sayings).
4. Quran 3:42.
5. Quran 3:45–47.
6. "Anti-Muslim Sentiments Fairly Commonplace," Gallup, July 28, 2006, accessed June 28, 2013, http://www.gallup.com/poll/24073/antimuslim -sentiments-fairly-commonplace.aspx.

CHAPTER 4

1. Hadith: Muslim oral traditions of the Prophet's sayings.
2. Drew Desilver, "World's Muslim Population More Widespread than You Might Think," PewResearchCenter, June 7, 2013, accessed September 4, 2013, www.pewresearch.org/fact-tank/2013/06/07/worlds-muslim-population -more-widespread-than-you-might-think/.
3. Mehran Kamrava, *The New Voices of Islam* (Berkeley: University of California Press, 2006), 155.
4. Ibid.
5. Rumi, "Daylight: A Daybook of Spiritual Guidance," accessed September 20, 2013, http://blog.gaiam.com/quotes/authors/mevlana-rumi?page=20.
6. Stephanie Saldana, *The Bread of Angels: A Journey to Love and Faith* (New York: Doubleday, 2010), 96.

CHAPTER 5

1. Mohammad Ayatollahi Tabaar, "Who Wrote the Koran?," *New York Times*, December 5, 2008, accessed June 1, 2013, www.nytimes.com/2008/12/07 /magazine/07wwln-essay-t.html.
2. Ibid.
3. Ibid.
4. Ibid.
5. Samuel P. Huntington, "The Clash of Civilizations?" *Foreign Affairs*, 1993.

★ NOTES ★

CHAPTER 6

1. Hadith: Muslim oral traditions of the Prophet's sayings.
2. Colin Powell, interview, *Meet the Press,* NBC, October 20, 2008.
3. Franklin Graham, interview, *Face the Nation,* CBS, February 21, 2012.
4. Justin Elliot, "Muslim Republican Heckled as Terrorist," *Salon,* September 27, 2011, accessed December 3, 2012, www.salon.com/2011/09/27/florida _gop_rejects_muslim/.

CHAPTER 7

1. "#226–Friday Sermon on QatarTV: With Some Women, Life Is Impossible Unless You Carry a Rod," *MemriTV,* August 27, 2004, accessed August 1, 2013, http://www.memritv.org/clip/en/226.htm.
2. Quran 3:7.
3. Neil MacFarquhar, "Verse in Koran on Beating Wife Gets a New Translation," *New York Times,* March 25, 2007, accessed July 2, 2013, http://www .nytimes.com/2007/03/25/world/americas/25iht-koran.4.5017346.html?page wanted=all&_r=0.
4. Ahmed Ali, *Al-Qur'an: A Contemporary Translation,* bilingual ed. (Princeton, NJ: Princeton University Press, 2001).
5. Iftikar Al-Bendari, "Husband Beating Fatwa," *Onislam,* October 27, 2008, accessed November 7, 2012, http://onislam.net/english/news/global/423581 .html.
6. Steve Englebright, "Legislation Strengthening New York's Domestic Violence Laws Passes Legislature," Assembly District 4, June 12, 2012, accessed August 1, 2013, http://assembly.state.ny.us/mem/Steve-Englebright/story/48482/.

CHAPTER 8

1. Lady Evelyn Cobbold, *Pilgrimage to Mecca* (London: Arabian Publishing, 2009).
2. This portion of my interview was not actually aired, as it was edited out in post. The program aired October 1, 2010, http://abcnews.go.com/2020/video /islam-questions-answers-11781366.

CHAPTER 9

1. Ahlam Mosteghanemi, *Memory in the Flesh (Modern Arabic Writing)* (Cairo: American University in Cairo Press, 1985), 15.

2. Hassan Hassan, "Million's Poet Finalist Defies Death Threats," *The National*, March 19, 2010, accessed September 4, 2013, http://www.thenational.ae /news/uae-news/millions-poet-finalist-defies-death-threats.

CHAPTER 10

1. Tom Robbins, "NYPD Cops' Training Included an Anti-Muslim Horror Flick," *Village Voice*, January 19, 2011.
2. Associated Press, "Protests over Anti-Muslim Film Continue with Scores Hurt in Bangladesh," *Guardian*, September 22, 2012, http://www.theguardian .com/world/2012/sep/22/protests-anti-muslim-film.
3. Gillian Flaccus, "Anti-Muslim Film Promoter Outspoken on Islam," AP, September 13, 2012, accessed June 12, 2013, bigstory.ap.org/article/anti -muslim-film-promoter-outspoken-islam.
4. Serge F. Kovaleski and Brooks Barnes, "From Man Who Insulted Muhammad, No Regret," *New York Times*, November 26, 2012.

CHAPTER 11

1. Martin Peretz, "The New York Times Laments 'A Sadly Wary Misunderstanding of Muslim-Americans.' 'But Really Is It 'Sadly Wary' or A 'Misunderstanding' At All?," *New Republic*, September 4, 2010, accessed April 1, 2013, http://www.newrepublic.com/blog/77475/the-new-york-times-laments -sadly-wary-misunderstanding-muslim-americans-really-it-sadly-w.
2. Quran 5:44.
3. "Message Delivered by Imam Feisal Abdul Rauf," February 23, 2003, accessed March 3, 2013, http://www.bj.org/wp-content/uploads/2010/08/daniel _pearl_memorial.pdf.
4. "Bloomberg on Mosque: 'A Test of Our Commitment to American Values,'" *Wall Street Journal*, accessed February 3, 2013, http://blogs.wsj.com/ metropolis/2010/08/24/bloomberg-on-mosque-a-test-of-our-commitment -to-american-values/.

CHAPTER 12

1. "The Innocence of Muslims," *TheMohammedFilms*, September 16, 2012, accessed November 11, 2012, http://www.youtube.com/watch?v=JsIqjg3VkrE& bpctr=1380582568.
2. Palash Ghosh, "Hillary Clinton Condemns Anti-Islam Film (FULL TEXT)," *International Business Times*, September 13 2012, http://www.ibtimes.com /hillary-clinton-condemns-anti-islam-film-full-text-788950.

CHAPTER 13

1. Dave Zirin, "The Slandering of NY Jet Oday Aboushi," *The Nation*, July 11, 2013, accessed September 4, 2013, www.thenation.com/blog/175216/slander -ny-jet-oday-aboushi#axzz2YqVlzBXn.
2. Tom Chivers, "Please be Quiet, Richard Dawkins, I'm Begging, as a Fan," *The Telegraph*, August 8, 2013, accessed September 4, 2013, blogs.telegraph .co.uk/news/tomchiversscience/100230250/please-be-quiet-richard-dawkins -im-begging-as-a-fan/.
3. Sam Harris, "In Defense of Profiling," *The Blog*, April 28, 2012, accessed April 14, 2013, www.samharris.org/blog/item/in-defense-of-profiling.
4. "'No Muslim Parking' Signs Spark Outrage," CNN, August 9, 2013, accessed September 1, 2013, religion.blogs.cnn.com/2013/08/09/no-muslim-parking -signs-spark-outrage/comment-page-17/.
5. Nick Wing, "Mike Huckabee: Muslims Depart Mosques Like 'Uncorked Animals,' Throwing Rocks, Burning Cars," *Huffington Post*, August 8, 2013, accessed September 4, 2013, www.huffingtonpost.com/2013/08/08/mike-huck abee-muslims_n_3725678.html.

CHAPTER 14

1. Susan Wise Bauer, *The Story of the World: History for the Classical Child*, rev. ed., Vol. 2 (Charles City, VA: Peace Hill Press, 2007), 62.
2. Maria Rosa Menocal, *The Ornament of the World* (New York: Little, Brown and Company, 2002).

CHAPTER 15

1. Cyril Glasse, *The Concise Encyclopedia of Islam*, rev. ed. (London: Stacey International, 2001), 141.
2. Quran 5:32.
3. Quran 2:190-193.
4. Quran 109:6.
5. Dr. Jamal Badawi, "Is Apostasy a Capital Crime in Islam," *The Fiqh Council of North America*, accessed September 23, 2013, http://www.fiqhcouncil.org /node/34.
6. Michael Finkel, "Facing Down the Fanatics," *National Geographic Magazine*, October 2009, accessed May 3, 2013, http://ngm.nationalgeographic.com /print/2009/10/indonesia/finkel-text.

CHAPTER 17

1. Nadine al-Bedair, "'My Four Husbands and I': Saudi Journalist Argues Women Should Have Right to Practice Polygamy Like Men," *Care2MakeaDifference*, January 6, 2010, accessed August 14, 2013, http://www.care2.com/causes/my -four-husbands-and-i-saudi-journalist-argues-women-should-have-right-to -practice-polygamy-like-men.html.
2. Khaled Diab, "Polygamy for All," *Guardian*, January 2, 2010, accessed June 1, 2013, http://www.theguardian.com/commentisfree/belief/2010/jan/02/poly gamy-polyandry.
3. Adrian Blomfield, "Egypt Purges Niqab from Schools and Colleges," *Telegraph*, October 5, 2009, accessed December 13, 2012, http://www.telegraph .co.uk/news/worldnews/africaandindianocean/egypt/6262819/Egypt-purges -niqab-from-schools-and-colleges.html.

CHAPTER 18

1. Maggie Fazeli Fard, "Sandra Fluke, Georgetown Student Called a 'Slut' by Rush Limbaugh, Speaks Out," *Washington Post*, March 2, 2012, accessed May 3, 2013, http://www.washingtonpost.com/blogs/the-buzz/post/rush-limbaugh -calls-georgetown-student-sandra-fluke-a-slut-for-advocating-contraception /2012/03/02/gIQAvjfSmR_blog.html.
2. Philip Pullella, "Pope Francis Reiterates 'Radical Feminist' Criticism of US Nuns' Group," Reuters, April 15, 2013.
3. "The Global Muslim Women's Shura Council: Vision, Missions and Objectives," www.wisemuslimwomen.org/about/shuracouncil/.

CHAPTER 19

1. "Abba Eban, the Father of Israeli Statesmanship, Dies at the Age of 87," *Facts ofIsrael.com*, November 18, 2002, accessed June 1, 2013, http://www.factsof israel.com/blog/archives/000491.html.
2. "Palestinians Attack Mitt Romney for 'Racist' Comments," BBC, July 30, 2012, accessed September 4, 2013, www.bbc.co.uk/news/world-us-canada-190 55643.

CHAPTER 20

1. Lizzy Ratner, "The War between Civilized Man and Pamela Gellar," *The Nation*, October 18, 2012, accessed November 18, 2013, http://www.thenation .com/article/170663/war-between-civilized-man-and-pamela-geller.

★ NOTES ★

2. Samuel P. Huntington, "The Clash of Civilizations?" *Foreign Affairs* 72, no. 3 (Summer 1993): 22–49.
3. Tom Heneghan, "Merkel: Germany Doesn't Have 'Too Much Islam,' but 'Too Little Christianity," Reuters, November 15, 2010, accessed September 24, 2013, blogs.reuters.com/faithworld/2010/11/15.
4. Ben Moreell, "Religion & Liberty," *Acton Institute,* http://www.acton.org/pub /religion-liberty/volume-2-number-6/power-corrupts.

CHAPTER 21

1. Jonathan Curiel, *Al' America: Travels through America's Arab and Islamic Roots* (New York: New Press, 2008), 8.
2. Khaled Abou El Fadl, *The Search for Beauty in Islam* (Lanham, MD: Rowman & Littlefield, 2006), 1.
3. Ibid.
4. Quran 17:36.
5. Quran 3:7.
6. Quran 1:7.
7. El Fadl, *Search for Beauty in Islam,* 22.

CHAPTER 22

1. Pete Winn, "Mentions of 'God' in Party Platform, Republicans 12, Democrats 0," CNS News, September 4, 2012, accessed September 4, 2013, cnsnews .com/news/article/mentions.

INDEX